Alexander Balloch Grosart, Giles Fletcher

Poems

Alexander Balloch Grosart, Giles Fletcher

Poems

ISBN/EAN: 9783744710657

Printed in Europe, USA, Canada, Australia, Japan

Cover: Foto ©Thomas Meinert / pixelio.de

More available books at **www.hansebooks.com**

The Fuller Worthies' Library.

THE

POEMS

OF

GILES FLETCHER, B.D.,

RECTOR OF ALDERTON, SUFFOLK:

FOR THE FIRST TIME

COLLECTED AND EDITED:

WITH

Memorial-Introduction and Notes:

BY THE

REV. ALEXANDER B. GROSART,

ST. GEORGE'S, BLACKBURN, LANCASHIRE.

PRINTED FOR PRIVATE CIRCULATION.
1868.

156 COPIES ONLY.

TO

A. J. Symington, Esq.,

GLASGOW:

A

·Sweet Singer;·

A

'Warbler of Poetic Prose;'

AND A

Good and True Friend;

THIS FIRST COLLECTED EDITION OF AN OLD

POET IS

AFFECTIONATELY DEDICATED

BY

ALEXANDER B. GROSART.

in London by the testimony of Thomas Fuller in
his 'Worthies.'* His informant was the Rev.
John Ramsey of 'Rougham in Norfolk' who
married the widow of our Poet.† It is to be
regretted that his birth-date was not given by
Fuller. Chalmers' ‡ conjecture of 1588 seems
improbable, as in the present volume will be found
his 'Canto' upon the death of Elizabeth, originally
published in 1603, that is, in such case, when he
was in his 14th or 15th year. I do not forget

---

* Vol. ii., 82 (edt. 1811 by Nichols).

† Fuller and after him his editors, and even Willmott,
  misspell this excellent man's name 'Rainsey.' It is
  Ramsey, as appears by a volume of his 'Sermons,' of
  ripe learning and rare quaintness and memorableness
  of thinking and style—which is in my library viz:
  'Præterita or a Summary of several Sermons: the
  greater part preached many years past in several
  places, and upon sundry occasions. By John Ramsey,
  Minister of East Rudham in the County of Norfolk,
  1650 (4°) The 'Registers' of his Church and Parish
  are all gone till within a century of the present time;
  and hence no memorial of him remains there. I have
  not met with another copy of his 'Præterita.' In his
  Epistle Dedicatory to Duport, he describes it as a
  'second mite into the Churches Treasury: the common
  gazophylacium of the Press.'

‡ Biog. Dict. *sub nomine.*

that at the same age, if not younger, Milton put forth "the shooting of the infant oak which in later times was to overshadow the forest"—as Dr. SYMMONS with unwonted vivacity describes his translations from the Psalms. But while these Psalms owe perhaps their choicest epithets and most vivid touches to Sylvester ('du-Bartas') the 'Canto' is strictly original and altogether too prodigious a production for a mere youth. The reader can turn to the 'Canto' and judge for himself.

Our first new fact—and a valuable one—we are able to add here viz : that his mother's name was JOAN SHEAFE of CRANBROOK, Kent, daughter of one of the wealthy clothiers of the place. The 'Register' shews that the marriage of this 'fair lady' with GILFS FLETCHER Senr., took place on 16th January, 1580 (o.s.) that is 1581.*

---

* I must heartily acknowledge the ungrudging labour of Mr. WILLIAM TARBUTT of CRANBROOK, in aiding my Fletcher-researches. Painstaking, persevering and intelligent, without pretence, Mr. TARBUTT is an enthusiast in all that honours his native town. We trust he will one day give us a 'History' of it. Mr. TARBUTT's investigations have yielded me important contributions to the Memoir of PHINEAS FLETCHER and the Family generally : of which more hereafter.

It is to be noted that Anthony a-Wood gives a place of honour to the son of Thomas Sheafe of Cranbrook, viz : Dr. Thomas Sheafe, who lies in the Chapel of St. George's, Windsor. In all probability this dignitary was brother of Joan, mother of our two poets.* What would we not give to have the mother of John Milton as certainly traced ?

FULLER further states that at an early age he was sent to 'Westminster' School, and that he was elected from it to Trinity College, Cambridge. On this WILLMOTT—than whom few have been more painstaking, as none had more penetrative insight, or finer poetic sympathies, or a more unerring taste—remarks:—

" This is the relation of Fuller; but I am unable to reconcile it with the declaration of GILES FLETCHER himself. In the dedication of 'Christ's Victorie' to Dr. NEVIL, he speaks, with all the ardour of a young and noble heart, of the kindness he had experienced from that excellent man. He mentions his having reached down 'as it were out of heaven, a benefit of that nature and price,

---

* Athenæ Oxon: by Bliss, *sub nomine:* his censure of another related SHEAFE for leaving his money to 'laymen' and not the Church, is mere abuse, and utterly unwarranted.

than which he could wish none (only heaven itself excepted) either more fruitful and contenting for the time that is now present, or more comfortable and encouraging for the time that is already past, or more hopeful and promising for the time that is yet to come." And further on, he expressly states that he was placed in Trinity College by Dr. Nevil's 'only favour, most freely, without either any means from others, or any desert in himself.' This praise could not have been consistent with truth, if Fletcher had obtained his election from Westminster School; and a careful examination of the Register-Book enables me to add that he was not upon the Foundation."*

This is decisive; and yet no one will bear hard on dear FULLER, with such a mass of material to assort. I can testify, after following him in many recondite and special lines of inquiry, that his general accuracy is not less amazing than his immense industry.

---

* Lives of the English Sacred Poets: by Robert Aris Willmott. 2nd edition, 2 vols. 12mo. 1839: Vol I. p 64. This is preferable here to the first edition, as it corrects previous errors, and is fuller: but the first edition is preferable in other respects, as will appear.

The patronage of Dr. NEVIL must have been
well-timed; for through the paternal responsibilities
incurred as executor of his Bishop-brother, the
Family were enduring at the period, painful hard-
ships as an extant Letter—elsewhere to be used—
gives pathetic evidence *

That the ' Canto ' of young Master GILES found
so prominent a place in so prominent a volume as
' Sorrowe's Joy ' : wherein the ' wisest Fool ' King
JAMES, was welcomed by nearly all the University
' singers ', including PHINEAS FLETCHER—would
seem to argue premature recognition. And yet
very slender are the records of him even in his
own College—renowned Trinity. Cooper's ATHENÆ
CANTABRIGIENSIS strangely fails us altogether,
though already covering the years of GILES' attend-
ance.†   Wood's ATHENÆ designates him ' bat-
chelour of divinity of Trinity College,' and adds
with rare feeling for him "equally beloved of the
muses and graces."‡ Does the mention of the

---

* See our Memoir of Phineas: and meanwhile Bond's
    ' Preface' to Dr. Fletcher's book on Russia, pp. cxxv
    —vi.

† Vol. I. 1500—85 : Vol. II. 1586—1609. Are we never
    to get Vol. III ?

‡ Fasti (by Bliss) I. 190—191.

'Graces' point to his personal beauty? If so—
it recalls the 'comeliness' and noble presence of
his uncle (Bishop FLETCHER) that so 'took'
Elizabeth.

We are enabled to add to his TRINITY dates.
In the Scholars' Admission Book is the following
entry in his own handwriting, under 'April 12th,
1605.'

'Ægidius Fletcherus, Dicipulus juratus.'

His name also occurs among the B.A. scholars
in the Senior Bursar's book for 1606. He is
there shewn to have received two quarterly payments of 3s. 4d. The book for 1605 is missing,
as is that for 1607 ; but in 1608 his name appears
as a B.A. scholar, and he receives four quarterly
payments of 3s. 4d. Such is all of 'Register'-
memorial left ; slight but all new facts. *

There can be no doubt that from 1603 of the
'Canto,' to 1610 he was laying up those stores of
various learning and of scholastic Divinity, for
which he was afterwards so remarkable.

In 1610, he published the poem—'Christ's
Victorie'—on which his Fame will rest immovably

---

* I am deeply indebted to MR. W. ALDIS WRIGHT, M.A.,
of Trinity College for discovering these entries for me.

' while there is any praise.'* A second edition
was not issued until 1632. It is sufficiently clear
that no more than the immortal ' Folio' of 1623,
'Paradise Lost' or 'Silex Scintillans' was this
consummate poem 'popular' while from his
brother's Lines it is evident that 'malicious
tongues' depreciated it; and that otherwise he
was not sufficiently estimated. We must here
read the loving fraternal 'Lines.' "Upon my
brother Mr. G. F. his book entituled ' Christ's
Victorie and Triumph.'   .   :

Fond lads, that spend so fast your posting time,
(Too posting time, that spends your time as fast)
To chant light toyes, or frame some wantom rhyme,
Where idle bôyes may glut their lustfull taste;
Or else with praise to clothe some fleshly slime
With virgin roses and fair lilies chaste;
　　While itching blouds and youthfull eares adore it;
But wiser men, and once yourselves, will most abhorre it.

But thou (most neare, most deare) in this of thine
Hast prov'd the Muses not to Venus bound;
Such as thy matter, such thy Muse, divine;
Or thou such grace with Mercie's self hast found,
That she herself deignes in thy leaves to shine;

Or stoll'n from heav'n, thou brought'st this verse to
  ground,
Which frights the nummèd soul with fearfull thunder,
And soon with honeyed dews thawes it 'twixt joy and
  wonder.

Then do not thou malicious tongues esteem ;
(The glasse, through which an envious eye doth gaze,
Can eas'ly make a mole-hill mountain seem)
His praise dispraises, his dispraises praise ;
Enough, if best men best thy labours deem,
And to the highest pitch thy merit raise ;
  While all the Muses to thy song decree
Victorious Triumph, triumphant Victorie.," 1

That 'Christ's Victorie' had one supreme 'student'
in JOHN MILTON every one discerns; and the
'one' is compensating renown. Surely and perma-
nently, if slowly, the majority came round to the
'one;' and now whoever knows aught of English
Literature, knows 'by heart' the 'thoughts that
breathe in words that burn' of this truly divine
and imperishable Poem. If GILES had lived to see
his brother's 'Siccelides' (1631); and perchance
he did see it in the Manuscript—he would
doubtless have found cheer in these lines of the,

---

1. ' Poeticall Miscellaniess,' p.p. 101-102 (1633).

' Epilogue' in answer to the question ' What euer
feast could every guest content?' viz :

> " In this thought, this thought the Author eas'd
> Who once made all, all rules—all neuer pleas'd ;
> FAINE WOULD WE PLEASE THE BEST, IF NOT THE MANY
> AND SOONER WILL THE BEST BE PLEASED THEN ANY;
> OUR REST WE SET IN PLEASING OF THE BEST,
> So wish we you what you may give us : Rest."

Fuller has neglected to inform us in what year
our 'sweet Singer' received ordination; but while
in residence at Cambridge he was much sought
after as a 'preacher.'   His pulpit was sacred ' St.
Mary's' from which have come perhaps the grandest
Sermons ever spoken by mortal tongues, and to
the most large-brained auditories found anywhere,
not excepting 'Paule's Crosse.' *   A peculiarity
of his 'prayers,' was that they usually consisted of
one entire allegory ' not driven, but led on, most
proper in all particulars." †   It is scarcely a loss
that 'prayers' of this type have not been preserved,
and yet one would have liked to see a specimen,
as one rejoices that in sequestered places one may

---

* Cf. my Memoir of Dr. Richard Sibbes, Vol I. pp. lii,
   liii : and Masson's ' Milton.'
† Fuller, as before.

still see Gardens of the antique sort, wherein the God-made sylvage is transformed by art into all manner of Dutch fantastiques of beds and knots, ' without a leaf astray,' as 'Our Village' describes.

In '1612' Fletcher edited and published at Cambridge the 'Remains' of a remarkable 'Oxford' man—NATHANIEL POWNOLL. The 'Epistle Dedicatory' is addressed to John King, Bishop of London.;* and is a bit of terse, thoughtful English. Willmot laments that he had not been able to obtain the book as "it would certainly tend to illustrate the poet's history." Between the first edition of his 'Lives' (1834) and the second (1839) he seems to have despaired of ever seeing it, and drops out all mention of it.† I am very pleased to be able to produce it from SELDEN's copy

---

* See my Memoir of Bishop King prefixed to reprint of his 'Jonah' [4to.]

† Cf. the former, p. 34 : In a foot-note here, WILLMOTT is perplexed with a contradiction between WATT's 'Bibliotheca Brittannica' and the antiquary COLE, because the former describes Pownoll's volume as printed at 'Canterbury' : but the explanation is that there was a mistake of Watt's editors (for his work was posthumous) in reading Cant[abrigiæ]:=Cambridge, as Canterbury.

of PowNOLL, preserved in the ' Bodleian '*   Here
it is :—

    ' To the Reverend Father in God John L[ord]
       Bishop of London.

Right woorthie and reuerend Father in God :

Blame not your ancient Obseruer, if nowe, after
he hath recouered in a manner, at Cambridge, that
life which he lost at his departure from Oxford,
he rises aniew, as it wear out of his ashes, to do
his humble seruice to his Lordship ; and, indeede,
to whome can any fruit that comes from him, bee
with more right presented then to him, in whose
garden, and onder whose shadow it griew ? Into
whose hand should this small book, though
wanting his owne Epistle, be deliuered, but onto

---

* The following is the full title-page ' The Young Divines
   Apologie for his continuance in the Universitie with
   Certaine Meditations, written by Nathaniel Pownoll,
   late student of Christ- Church in Oxford.   Printed by
   Cantrell Legge, Printer to the Vniversitie of Cam- .
   bridge ; and are to be sold in Paul's Churchyard by
   Matthew Lownes at the signe of the Bishop's head,'
   1612, [12mo.] Another edition of the 'Young Divine's
   Apology' was published at Oxford in 1658 'printed
   for T. Robinson' and to this are added (1) His
   Meditation upon the calling of the Ministrie at his

that, to which it hath before given so many Epistles? whear can it looke for protection with more hope then whear it hath formerly, with all fauour founde it? If your Lordship thearfore will be pleased to be the defender of this Apologie, and to breath as I may truly say, the breath of life againe into his sequent Meditations, that so beeing annimated aniew with those onspeakable sighs, and alike feruent zeale of spirit, wherwith they wear first, as in fierie chariots, carried up into heau'n; I doubt not but they will seeme, beeing so quickned, to any that shall reade them (especially if, as Job wished in a case not much onlike, his soule wear in his soules stead) no cold, or dull, or dead

first institution unto it. (2) A Meditation upon the first of the seauen penitentiall Psalmes of David. (3) His daily Sacrifice. These last three are contained in one volume at the end of the 'Apologie' 1612. I notice that in the Will of our Giles' Uncle—Bishop RICHARD FLETCHER—he bequeaths, among other things the following: 'Item,' I geue vnto my sister Pownoll twenty poundes. (Dyce's Beaumont & Fletcher, Vol. I. lxxxviii.) Was this the mother of our Pownoll? If so then we have a key to our poet's interest in editing and publishing his 'Remaines': in such case he was his cousin.

lettets; and in so doing, you shall not onely follow
him into his graue, but call him out of it with
this so speciall a benefit, binding with the dead in
one knot of thankfulnesse all his friends that yet
live, and cannot but ioy to see your Lordship's
fauour out-live the person on whom it is bestowed:
of whome my selfe, being the leaste, shal euer
thinke I am most bound to be.

Your L. to command in all good seruice

G. FLETCHER.'

To this falls to be added an equally good 'Epistle'
to 'the Reader' which follows :—

' The Authour of this small discourse, or rather
(giue mee leaue so to call him) the Swan that,
before his death, sung this diuine song, is now
thear, whear he neither needs the praise, nor
fears the envy of any: whose life, as it deserued
so it was covetous of no mans commendation ;
himselfe being as farre from pride as his desert was
neere it, yet because it was his griefe, that hee
should die before he was fit to doe God the seruice
hee desired ; and his friends desire, that beeing so
fit as hee was for his service, hee might (if it had
been possible) neuer have died at all ; thearfore
his booke was bould to thrust itselfe into that
world which the Author of it had lately left, thereby

to .satisfye both his Makers desire, in doing tho church of God some scruice; and his friends griefe, in not suffering him altogether to lic dead..

And truely what better seruice can it doe, then to persuade with reason, since Authoritie forces not, our young Neophytes to abide awhile in the schooles of the Prophets, at Bethel, before they presume to enter the Temple at Hierusalem ; and if reason can doe little with them, because happily they want it, yet let his example (an argument that prevails much with the common people, of whome such prophets are the tayle) make them at least see, and confesse, though they know not how to amend, their fault. Ten yeares had hee liued in the Uniuersitie, eight languages had hee leart, and taught his tongue so many scueral waies by which to expresse a good heart; watching often, daily exercising, alway studying, in a word, making an end of himselfe in an ouer-feruent desire to benefit others; and yet, after hee had, as it wear out of himself, sweat out all this oyle for his lampe, after hee had with the sunne ran so many heauenly races, and when the sunne was laied abed by his labours, after hee had burnt out so many candles to giue his minde light (hauing alwaies S. Paul's querie in his minde τις προς ταυτα ικανος) hee neuer durst adventure

to doe that, after all these studies done, and ended,
which our young novices, doeing nothing, eoumpt
nothing to doe: but still thought himselfe as
unfit, as hee kniew all men weare nnworthy
of so high an honour, as to be the Angells of God.

I could wish that he had left behinde him, if
not all his learning, yet some of his modesty to
be diuided among these empty sounding vessels,
that want both; but since in him so great
examples of piety, knowledge, industrie, and
unaffected modesty are all fallen so deeply asleep,
as I am afraid we shall hardly find in any of his
age the like, (which I speak not to deny iust
praise to the liuing; but who will not afford a
fiew flowers to strowe the cophine of the dead?)
thear was no way to awaken them, and in them
him, but by layeing them up, not with him in his
grauc, but in these immortal monuments of the
presse, the liuing Tombes proper to dead learning,
wherein these flowers may liue, though their roote
be withered, and though the trunke be dead, the
branches flowuish.

Let rich men therefore in the guilded sepulchres
and proud monuments of their death, beg for tho
memory of their liues: the righteous shall be had
in euerlasting remembrance, without any such
proud beggary; nor shall he euer be beholding to

a dead stone for the matter; and good reason, Righteousness being a shadow of that divine substance, which hath in it no shadow of change much less of corruption : only I could wish their liues wear as long as their memories; that so this crooked age might haue as great store, as it hath need of them.

G. F.

Prefixed to the 'Bodleian' copy of Pownoll is this Latin M.S. Epitaphum.

> ' Flos juvenum, decus Oxonii, spes summa parentum
>   Te tegit ante diem (matre parante) lapis.—
> Hoc satis est cineri : reliqua immortalia coelo
>   Condit amorque hominum, condit amorque Dei.'

When our FLETCHER left CAMBRIDGE is not known; but probably it was shortly after 1610, the year of the publication of his Poem and also of the death of his Father—who it is to be feared did not live to read 'Christ's Victorie,' in print at least. That he was a Divinely-'called' not merely Bishop-ordained 'minister of the Gospel' is certain. For in the invocation of his great Poem he adoringly acknowledges *the* one mighty change within, the gentle yet awful dower that alone warrants a man to accept the august office. As PHINEAS has like definite and deep words con-

cerning the same central thing—which will duly
appear in his Memoir—it would almost seem as
though the two brothers were moved, inclined,
and enabled to give themselves to their Lord at
the same time. With hush of awe, not without
white tears, one reads the goldenly precious self-
revelation, modest but frank, frank because con-
fiding. They must find place here :

...... " The obsequies of Him that could not die
    And death of life, ende of eternitie,
How worthily He died, that died vnworthily ;......
    Is the first flame wherewith my whiter Muse
    Doth burne in heauenly love, such love to tell.
    O Thou that didst this holy fire infuse,
    Aud taught'st this brest, *but late the graue of hell,*
    Wherein a blind, and dead heart liu'd, to swell
        With better thoughts, send downe those lights that
            lend
        Knowledge, how to begin, and how to end
    The loue, that neuer was, nor euer can be pend.' *

Thus baptized with Fire 'from the Altar' he became
a servant-Shepherd under the Owner-shepherd.

    FULLER says " He was at last (by exchange of
his living) settled in Suffolk." On this WILLMOTT
observes " It seems improbable that he would

---

* Part I., s. 1, 3.......

have relinquished any other preferment for a
situation which is supposed to have hastened the
period of his death;" and he continues "[He]
did not live long to reap the advantage of his
preferment; the unhealthiness of the situation
combined with the ignorance of his parishoners, to
depress his spirits and exhaust his constitution ;
a lonely village in the maritime part of Suffolk,
more than two hundred years ago, had few conso-
lations to offer to one accustomed to the refined
manners and elegant occupations of an University.
We are told by Fuller in the quaint manner for
which he is remarkable, that Fletcher's ' clownish
and low-parted parishioners (having nothing but
their shoes high about them) valued not their
pastor according to his worth, which disposed him
to melancholy and hastened his dissolution.' "*

---

* As before, p. 67 : " He may have been " suggests Willmott here, "presented to the living by Sir Robert
   Naunton, whose family were the patrons of the Church
   and had their residence in the parish. Naunton was
   Public Orator during several years of Fletcher's
   residence at Cambridge, and being himself a member
   of Trinity was, probably, well acquainted with his
   poetry and genius."   On this, in a little Paper which
   appeared in the Ipswich Journal, (March 12th, 1853) a
   local Writer adds " If Scipio departed from Rome to

We are reminded of HERRICK's like experience
among his 'clownish' Devonshire parishioners.
Unfortunately the 'Registers' of ALDERTON—the
'living' of Fletcher—only go back to 1674; so
that there are no accessible records to get at
Facts and dates.

While 'Rector' I do not doubt he discharged
faithfully the functions of his office ; and his prose
in the form of 'Epistles' and 'Prefaces' already
given, and those which precede his Poem, should
alone warrant us in concluding that he had preach-
ing-power. But besides it is our rare happiness
to have before us a copy—believed to be unique—
of a prose treatise by our Worthy, that gives us in
all likelihood the substance of a series of sermons.
The title-page of this solitary copy is awanting;
and all search and re-search have failed to trace
another—but from the references to BACON under

---

fix his residence in some remote locality, it was but
natural that he should sigh for the companionship of
his beloved Lælius." It is discreditable in no common
degree to Suffolk that an appeal by the (then) Rector
for funds in order to place a marble tablet in the wall
of the 'old Rectory' in memory of Fletcher, remains
un-responded to and the pious project unperformed.
O Shame where is thy blush?

his title of 'Lord Verulam, Viscount Saint Albones,' it cannot have been earlier than 1621—the year of the creation of St. Albans—nor later than 1623, the year of its author's death.* As this Book has escaped the knowledge of all our Fletcher's previous Biographers, I shall give first of all the ' Epistle Dedicatory,' and thereafter extracts illustrative of its thought and style.

The ' Epistle'—as already noted—refers to 'favours' conferred by BACON. It is saddening that we cannot know more of their nature. Was it the 'presentation' to Alderton? and the graciousness of it? †

The ' Epistle ' is as follows :

'To the right Honorable and Religious, Sir Roger Townshend, Knight Baronet ;‡ all grace and peace.

---

* I owe my use of this precious volume to my accomplished friend George W. Napier, Esq., of Alderley Edge, near Manchester. It is daintily covered with satin and silver wire-work in flowers—which kind of binding is usually ascribed to the Nuns of Little Gidding.

† See Postscript at end of Memorial-Introduction.

‡ Sir John Townshend, Bart, M. P., married Anne, eldest daughter and co-heir of Sir Nathanael Bacon, K. B., half-brother of *the* Bacon. The eldest son of this marriage was the Roger of this Dedication,

Honourable Sir,

Benefits, they say, are alwayes best giuen when they are most concealed, but thanks when they are made most knowne. Giue my priuate estate leaue therefore to borrow the Art of the Printer, which is the publike Tongue of the learned, to expresse my selfe (though with no other learning then what your kinde respects haue taught mee) most gratefull vnto you: who indeed am bound, though principally, yet not onely to your Honoured selfe, but *totj Gentj tuæ*, to the worthy Lady your mother, the religious Knight, Sir Nathaniel, your second Father, & without thought, not beyond my desire, to your most noble & learned Vncle, the Right Honorable Francis Lord Verulam, Viscount Saint Albbnes, my free and very Honourable Benefactor, whose gift, as it was worthy his bestowing, so was it

---

created a Baronet in 1617. From him descend the present Marquis Townshend, Viscount Sydney, Baron Bayning, &c. (See 'Notes and Queries' 4th Series, May 23rd, 1868, p. 499). Phineas also dedicates his 'Locustæ' to Sir Roger, and his English 'Locusts' to Lady Townshend. See our edition of Phineas Fletcher, *in loco*. John Yates dedicates his 'Saints' Sufferings and Sinners' Sorrowes (1631) to Sir Roger Townsend, &c. G.

speedily sent, and not tediously sued for; Honourably giuen, not bought with shame, to one whom he neuer knew or saw, but onely heard kindly slaundered with a good report of others, and opinion conceiued by himselfe of sufficiencie and worth. For by your Fauours I confesse, my estate is something, but the sence of my pouertie much more increased. For if we may beleeue Neros wise Maister and Martyr; 'There is none so poore, as he who cannot requite a benefit:'* but I am glad your Estates will be alwayes beyond any retaliating † kindnesses of mine who could not, indeed, without doing you much iniury, wish my selfe able to make you amends.

As therefore Aristippus came to Dionysius, so doe I to you Ἐπὶ τῷ μεταδώσειν ὧν ἔχω καὶ μεταλήψεσθαι ὧν μὴ ἔχω Hauing received what I wanted, to returne what I had.‡ Though in trueth this small present may bee better sayed to bee giuen by you to others, then by my self to you, who thought it worthy of more mens reading then your owne,

---

* Seneca. G.

† An example of a now disused sense of this word, such as illustrates and confirms Trench's remarks on it in his well-known 'Study of Words.' G.

‡ Diogenes Laertius, *Vita Aristippi* ii. 77. G.

which I pray God it may be. Surely if there be
any worth in it, it is in the dignitie of the matter,
and the fitnesse of it, for our nature and times.
The matters are the Grounds, Exercise and Reward
of the faithfull, Heauenly Light, Bodily labour,
Spirituall rest. The first of which brings with it
light for our Soules; the second, Health for our
bodies, and the third for them both eternal
Blessednesse. But in our times there is three
vertues are so great strangers, in which there are
so many euill heartes of vnbeliefe, all standing
ready to depart from the liuing God, that wee
had need to offer a holy violence to our nature,
and to fall out with our times, that fall so fast
away from God, or else it is to be feared least the
tide and streame of them both carry vs not into the
riuers of Paradise, there to bee landed vpon the
mountaines of our saluation, but into the riuers of
Brimstone, whether all are wasted that depart
from God: as himselfe telleth vs; ' Depart from
mee yee cursed into euerlasting fire. '

And so much the more need had wee, that liue
in this last Age of the world, to looke to the infirmitie of our natures and diseases of the time:
because natural infirmities are alwayes greatest
Tyrants in our Age, and it is no otherwise in this
old world, then in old persons: If we were

borne weake sighted, it is a venture but in age a great dimnesse, if not a totall blindnesse doe not befall vs. If a lame hand by nature hath disabled the actions of our youth; the hand which in youth could doo little, will doe nothing in our age ; if we have traduced a personal inclination from our parents to any vice, it is a grace if that inclination grow not to an affection in our youth, and in our age to a habite. So fast grow the ill weedes of Nature when Nature it selfe decayes in vs.

Now wee cannot bee ignorant that in the very Spring of nature, these three strong infirmities were seeded in vs. The first vpon the effacing of Gods Image, a dimme eye-sight or darknesse in our soule : the second a lame hand or idlenesse in the body, which grew when Mortalitie first broke in vpon vs, and left our nature consumed of that first-borne strength it then flowrished with : bringing in vpon our labour an accursed sweat, vpon our sweat, wearinesse, and consequently faynting, and languishing the whole body with vnrest, and disease: The third vpon the losse of our heavenly inheritance, an inclination and affection of the whole man to such a happinesse, as wee cannot build for our selues, out of the beautie and delights of this world: which Salomon happily alluded vnto Eccles. 3. 11. where speaking

of Humane happinesse, to reioyce, and doe good,
that is, to eate and to drinke, and to enioy the good
of all our Labour, verse, 3, (Which questionlesse is
therefore lawfull, because it is there sayd to bee the
gift of God) hee telleth vs; that, 'God hath made
every thing beautifull in his season, and hath set
הָעֹלָם *cœlum*, the worlde, as it is translated, or the
desire of perpetuitie in their heartes, so that no
man can finde out the worke that God maketh
from the beginning to the end.' Whereas it seemes
to me, Salomon allowing vs this Humane felicitie,
as good in it selfe, yet secretly accuseth it (by
reason of the immoderate affection, and desire of
perpetuitie wee cast after it) for blinding the eye
of our consideration so farre, as thereby wee cannot
finde out the worke that God maketh from the
beginning to the end, which doub[t]lesse* can bee
no other then his worke of our Redemption,
purposed from all eternitie in Christ our Lord
who therefore as himself is called πρωτότοκος πάσης
κτίσεως, the first-borne of all creatures, so his
day is cald *Nouissimus Dierum*, the last of all
dayes, he onely being (as himselfe witnesseth) A
and Ω and the First† and the Last, the beginning of

---

* Misprinted 'doublesse.' G.
† Misprinted 'Frst.' G.

all things and the ende of all things Colos. I., * 15; and in this worke onely consists the knowledge of our perfit happines wherein is both perpetuitie and sufficiency, which work of Gods, most men therefore cannot finde out, because they acquiet their desires with this humane felicitie, and lie downe vnder Issachars blessing, which indeed, is but a cursory and viatorie happinesse, seruing vs onely for the time and by the way.

These then are the three great diseases of our soules, bodies, and persons: Blindnesse of Spirit, Idlenesse of Body, Loue and rest in the world; which the beginning of the world, made by corruption, naturall; and the Age of the world, by the second nature, and of custome, hath made delightfull to vs. And truely, if our owne experience did not teach vs how most men in our daies placed themselues in these infirmities, and with what delight wee are ignorant, idle, and enamored of the world: yet the Oracles of God would plainely euidence it vnto vs, wherein wee shall finde it prophecied of this last tempest of the world, that it should bee full of seducing Spirits to infidelitie, of idle busie bodyes, of louers of pleasures more

---

* Misprinted '11.' G.

then louers of God.   To cure which three great
diseases * of our natures, and our times I haue
sent abroade by your perswasion (and therefore
haue burdened you with the Patronage of it)
this short Præscript, which I pray God may
worke by the power of his Spirit, soundnesse in
vs.   To the riches of whose grace, I most entirely
commend you, and rest Your Worships in all
hearty affection and Christian seruice

GILES FLETSHER.

I now proceed to select such portions of the
work itself—whose running title is "The Reward of
the Faithfull" from texts enumerated below†—as
have arrested my attention in reading it.   Taken as
a whole it is scarcely worthy of a reprint; but
our gleanings will, it is believed, interest.   The
'verse' bits will be found in their own place
among the poems.   ‡ I submit our extracts *seriatim*
from the commencement to the close:

---

* Misprinted 'diseased.'   G.

† Matthew v., 6, 'They shall be satisfied,' p.p. 1-127;
   Genesis xxvi., 12, pp. 127-302; Acts x., 43, pp. 303-
   419; Epistle Dedicatory 6 leaves; the severall argu-
   ments [imperfect] 2 leaves.

‡ Mr. Napier's is the same copy referred to by Dr. Neale
   and Mr. Hazlitt.   It is remarkable that this prose treatise
   of our Poet should not have been known after Phineas's

(1) "So much almes, and often fasting & due payment of tithes, what goodnesse haue they, if the almes must bee trumpeted abroad, and the fast must set a sowre face vpon the matter, and the tithes must bee boasted of, and layed as it were in Gods dish, when he comes to pray before him in the Temple, as though God who giues him all, were beholding to him, for restoring him the tenth part of his owne?" (p. 9.)   Again :—

(2) "Now it is a speech of our Sauiour which it may bee euery man remembers, but few men marke, when after fourty dayes fast in the wildernesse, he was tempted to satisfie his hunger by making bread of stones, he answered, That man liu'd not by bread onely, but by euery Word that proceeded out of the mouth of God.   Which speech though a prophane Ignorant will perhaps *derisively**

---

well-known verses given onward. It is much to be desired that another copy containing the title-page may be forthcoming. Meantime it is scarcely ever safe to designate any book *unique*, e.g. after fully ten years waiting I have just happened on ZACHARY CATLIN's 'Hid Treasure,' and at same time his translation of Ovid—books I had despaired of ever recovering ; and so it may be in any case.

* Misprinted ' derisonly.'   G.

scoffe at, as thinking it impossible to liue by
words, yet such words as proceed out of the mouth
of God haue more vitall sweetnesse, and nourish-
able sap in them, than all his corne, and oyle, and
wine haue.   Was not the whole world made by
the word of God? Was not the soule of euery
reasonable creature made by the same word, and so
imbreathed into the body of the first father of our
humane nature? and is now still infused into euery
one of our bodies, when they are perfectly
instrumented, and made fit for the soule to dwell
in?" (pp. 19—21.)   "Again :—

(3) " If a man digging in a field, find a mine,
we cal this fortune : but a mine must bee first
there by nature, before any can finde it there by
fortune.   And therefore fortune that comes
alwayes after nature, cannot bee the cause of
nature." (p. 24.)   Again :—

(4) " What nature in earth obserues the different motions of the heavenly bodies, and admires
the methodicall wisedom of God in them, and
thinkes vpon his couenant of mercy, when he
sees the token of it shining in the waterie cloud
(sweetly abusing the same waters to bee a token
of his mercy, which before were the instrument of
his iust revenge." (p. 30, 31.)   Again :

(5) " Whose eye lookes beyond the bright hilles of time, and there beholds eternity, or sees a spirituall world beyond this body, esteeming that farre discoasted region, his native country,* but onely man? (p. 31.)   Again :—

(6) So with the body. But we cannot drinke too much of our spirituall rocke, nor eate too much of our heauenly Manna, which after we haue feasted our hearts with, we shall find noe more hunger, or thirst; feele noe more iniuries of age, or time; feare noe more spoiles of mortality, or death. Neither is the soule nourished by this diuine food, as the body is, by wasting that whereby it selfe is preserued, and consuming that to maintaine it selfe, whereby it selfe is kept from corruption : but as the sight of al eyes is preserued and perfected by the light of the Sunne, whose beames can neuer be exhaust, so our spiritual life is nourished by the participation of the life of Christ which is indeed πηγάζων ζωὴ, annona cæli, the flower of heauen, neuer engrost by possessing, nor lost by vsing, nor wasted by nourishing, nor spent by enioying but hath that heauenly, and vnconsumable nature in it (being to nourish immortall soules) that it pre-

---

* Misprinted 'countey.'   G.

scrues al without decaying itselfe, it diuides it selfe to all without losse or diminution of it selfe; it is imparted to all and replenished, and not impayred by any of those soules that banquet vpon it." pp. 37—40.)   Again:—

(7) "Like the twilight of an euening, or the first breake of day in which the shadows of earth, and the light of heauen are confused." (p. 42.) Again:—

(8) "Makes vs of one spirit and one soule, as it were, with the Diuine being; not by the vnion of essence and information, but of inhabitance and participation." (p. 61.)   Again:—

(9) "But when the morning of glory shall arise, wherein our soules shall awaken from the heauy eye-lid of our flesh, and the veyle of our body shall first be remoued, and after being depur'd from his drosse, be refined into a bright and spirituall body, wee shall then see God as he is." (pp. 73, 74.) Again:—

(10) "So that looke as you see the very bright image of the Sunne so reflected vpon the water somtimes, that the dull Element seemes to haue caught downe the very glorious body it selfe, to paint her watry face with, and lookes more like a part of heauen, then like it selfe; who in the absence of the Sunne, is all sabled with blacknesse

and darknesse, and sad obscurity; but vpon tho first beames of the heauenly body, is glazed with a most noble & illustrious brightnesse; so is it with our whole man. For when God shall thus imprint and strike himselfe into our darke being, O how beautifull shall the feet of Gods saints bee? Esay 52. 7. What a Diadem of stars shall crowne their glorious heads? Reuelat. 12. How shall their amiable bodies shine in Sun-like Majesty? Mat. 13. 4." (pp. 77, 78.)   Again :—

(11) "This carried the heart of olde Simeon into such a holy extasie of religious delight, that earth could hold him no longer, but he must needs, as it were, breake prison, and leape out of his olde body into heauen. O what a desire of departure to it, doth a true sight of this saluation kindle! 'Lord,' saies he, 'now lettest,' &c. As if he should say, Lord, now the child is borne, let tho olde man die, now thy son is come, let thy seruant depart, now I haue seene thy salvation, O let mee goe to enioy it. Now I haue beheld the humanity of thy sonne, what is worth the looking vpon, but the diuinity of such a person, who is able to make my young Lord heere euen proud of his Humilitie. For so great a ioy of spirit can neuer be thrust vp into so small a Vessell, as an olde shrunke-vp body of earth is. Since therefore I

D

haue testified of thy Christ, since I haue made an
end of my dying note, and sung thee my Christ-
masse song; since I haue seene thee, O thou holy
one of Israell, whom no flesh can see & liue,
what haue I to do to liue, O Lord? What should
I weare this olde garment of flesh any more?
Thou hast left thy fatnesse off, O thou faire Oliue
Tree and the oyle of it hath made mee haue a
cheerefull countenance: thou hast forsaken thy
sweetnesse, O thou beautifull Vine, and thy fruit
hath warm'd thine olde Seruant at the very hart.
Now therfore being thou hast powred thy new
wine into this old vessell, O giue the olde bottle
leaue to breake, O let me depart in peace; for I
haue enough, I haue seen, mine eyes haue seene
thy saluation." (pp. 111—114.)   Again:—

(12) "Exod. 20. 9 . . . which is not to bee vnder-
stood as a Permission, but as a Precept: as though
God gaue vs onely leaue, & not charge to labour.
For hee sayes not, sixe daies thou Maist labour, but
six daies thou Shalt labour." (p. 131.)   Again:—

(13) " Are not al things imbrightned with vse,
and rustied with lying still? Let but the little
Bee become our mistresse. Is shee not alwaies
out of her artificiall Nature, either building her
waxen Cabinet, or flying abroad into the flowry
Meadowes or sucking honey from the sweete

plants, or loading her weake thighes with waxe to build with, or stinging away the theeuish Droan that would faine hiue it selfe among her labours, and liue vpon her sweete sweat? *Ignauum, fucos, pecus a præsepibus arcent.** And shal this Bittle creature, this Naturall goode hous wife thus set her selfe to her businesse, and shall we droano away our time in idlenesse, and which alwaies followes it, vicious liuing?" (pp. 138, 139.) Again :—

(14) It is indeede a naturall Truth, *Omne Corpus naturale quiescit in loco proprio.* Euery naturall body is quiescent in his owne proper place : and yet wee see though all gladly rest in their owne regions, and inuade not the confines of their neighbour Elements, yet they are alwayes mouing and coasting about in their owne orbes and circuits, thereby teaching vs to labour euery man in the circle of his owne calling, and not to busiebody out abroad with other newe workes. The Aire breakes not into the quarters of heauen and yet, wee see, it is alwayes fann'd from place to place, and neuer sleepes idly in his owne regions : the reason is, because otherwise it would soone putrifie

---

* Virgil. *Georg* iv. 168. G.

it selfe and poyson vs all with the stinking breath
of it, did not the diuine prouidence of God driue it
about the World with his Windes, that so it might
both preserue it selfe and serue to preserue us,
which otherwise it could neuer doe..........So
that in a word, euery thing moues for man, &
should man only himselfe be idle and stand still."
(pp. 143—146.)   More fully :—

(15) "A faithfull Minister is a great labourer. I
would not willingly make comparisons betweene
him and the husbandman, and say his labour is
beyond theirs; but this I may safely say, that
God himselfe compares him not onely to a husbandman, but to shew the greatnesse of his labour,
to euery calling indeed that is most sweated with
industrie and toyle. I know all men thinke their
owne callings most laborious, but whether thinke
you it easier to plow vpon hard ground, or vpon
hard stones? whether to commit your seed to
those furrowes that will return you fruitfull
thankes; or those that for your labor will spoyle
your seed, & requite you with reproch and
slander? whether to such ground as is good, and
naturally opens her bosome to drinke in the dewes
of heauen that fall upon her, and gladly receiues
the Sunne beames shed from God to warm and
make fruitfull the seede credited to her wombe,

or such ground as neuer thirsts after the watering
of Apollos, though as Moses speakes (Deut. 32. 2.)
his words drop as the raine, and his speech distill
as the dew; neuer can indure the light of heauen
to shine vpon it, but lies alwayes in darkenesse and
in the shadowes of death? yet such ground
(stones I should haue sayd) did the diuine courage of Stephen meet with in Ierusalem (Act. 7.
59), such S. Paul wronght on at Lystra (Act. 14
19.), such Moses and Aaron and Iosua toyled
vpon in the wildernes (Num. 14. 10.) such the
Prophets (Matt. 21, 25.) such the Prince of the
Prophets found in his owne inheritance, though
he had before (as we see in Esay 5. 2.) pickt
all the stones himselfe out of it (John 8, 59).
What one difficultie or danger is the roughest
calling assaulted with, that his is not. Does the
plowmans labour know no end, but is it˚ as the
Poet speakes of it :

> Labor actus in orbem,
> Quique in se sua per vestigia voluitur ? *

So is his. Does the Shepheard, the sun-burnt
and frosted shepheard, watch ouer his flockes

---

* More accurately "Redit agricolis labor actus in orbem,
Atque in se sua per vestigia rolvitur annus".—Virgil
Georg ii., 401-402. G.

by night, strengthen the diseased, set apart the
sound, binde vp the bruised, seek out the
lost, rescue those that are preyed vpon? So
does he.   Marches the soldier before the face
of death? liues hee among the pikes of a
thousand dangers? walks he throgh his owne
wounds and blood?   So does he: but as the
ground this spirituall plowman tils is ,harder,
so the wolves & Lyons this Shephcard watches
against are fiercer, and the Armies he graples
with of another temper then such as are made
like himselfe of flesh and blood; being Powers
and Principalities, spirituall wickednesses, &
worldly gouernors, one of whom could in a
nights space strike dead the liues of a hundred
fourescore and fiue thousand souldiers at once, all
armed and embattayld together Isay 37. 36. Let
all the Princes of valour that euer liued bring, into
the field their most tried and signall warriour,
whose face and brest stand thickest with the
honourable scarres* of braue aduentures; if I doe
not single out to encounter him one souldier
that beares in his body the markes of the Lord

---

* The original has 'honourable starres,' but 'markes'
 onward, shews it to be a misprint for 'scarres' as
 above. G.

Iesus, who shall haue broken through an Iliad of more daugers and perils, then he, let Gath and Ascalon triumph ouer Sion once againe, & let it be said that a second and more noble Saul is falne vpon his high places, then euer yet fell before. For wee shall finde him all the world ouer in labours more abundant, in iourneys more often, in more perils in the city, in the wilderness, in the sea, more often in watchings, and fastings, in hunger and thirst, in cold & nakednesse, in prison more frequent, and ofter in wearinesse and death 2 Cor. 11. 23. &c. Let not him therefore that sowes the earth with his labor, slander the spirituall tilth of our soules with lazie thoughts. Alas! in the time of peace contempt is the greatest haruest we reape and in the tempests of persecution, our blood is the first seed is sowne in the Church." (pp. 155—162.) Again :—

(16) " Isaac (1) a religious person sowes. (2) sowes in a time of famin and dearth (3) ground of strangers (4) reward." Again :—

(17) " What would one of our small heires say, should I now turne Farmour. I thanke God I haue beene brought vp after another fashion, and haue ground enough of mine owne to liue upon by other mens labours. Well I make no question

but Isaac was as well brought vp as such idle, out of calling gentlemen, and yet he plowes, and sowes, not only another mans ground, but the ground of straungers, where hee could expect nothing but hard dealing; which indeed hee found." (pp. 171, 172.)   Again :—

(18) " God........His are no Court-promises prodigally made, and purposely forgotten. (p. 177.) Again :—

(19) " All these mischiefes happen not to rich men, but to men that will bee rich, not to men that haue money but to men that loue money and set their heart vpon it. 'If riches increase,' &c., saies Dauid. A man may haue riches, but riches must not haue the man." (p. 183.)—

(20) " It may be thou art godly and poore. Tis well : but canst thou tell whether, if thou wert not poore, thou wouldst be godly ? Sure God knows vs better then wee ourselues doe, and therefore can best fit the estate to the person." (pp. 211, 212.)   Again :—

(21) " Rest therefore thy selfe content with that estate God hath set thee in, that is best for thee, if thou beest a childe of God, and it is not Gods order to giue thee his blessings to hurt thee with." (p. 212.)   Again :—

(22) "A covetous man is the poorest man aliue. For must not he needs be poore, whom God himselfe doth not satisfie?" (p. 218.)   Again :—

(23) "But indeed to say true. A couctous man that rauines and snatches at other mens goods is no more properly in Gods sight a rich man, then we would call him that had stollen a great summe of mony from another man, rich. We shall doe him no wrong if we call him a rich theefe. For yee know wee neuer reckon the goods of theeues their owne goods, because as soon as they are taken notice of, their goods are all seiz'd vpon to the Kings vse: And so many times as soone as God sends out his pale Pursiuant to attach this couctous wretch, the goods presently are disposed of, all [as] God will haue them: sometimes it may be to his honest heire, or perhaps to the destruction of such as inherit with his sinne his substance, as the rich Epulœs Brothers: but many times to the building of Hospitals or the erecting of Grammar Schooles, or putting out of Prentises or redeeming of Prisoners or founding of Colledges or releeuing of maimed Soldiers, or making of good waies, such as himselfe neuer walkt in (or which now is a rare point of pietie) in doing some good to the Church of God, by restoring to the right vse, vsurped and impropriate tithes, or buying

them from the dead hands they lie in, and laying
them vpon Gods Altar, that feedes not vnder the
Gospel any mortmaines, such as were the hands of
the Romane Clergie; but such as are more free, and
active in the seruice of the Prince, and Common-
wealth, then any in the whole bodie politique of
double their abilitie, and strength." (pp. 220—
223.)—

(24) " Gods love is the beginning, and thy
glory is the last end, the loue of God will bring
thee to : but there be many meanes betweene the
beginning and the ende, his loue and thy glory.
First, God's loue elects thee to be iustified, and to
worke thy iustification he cals thee, and that thou
maiest be called, he infuses into thy heart faith
in Christ, and that thou mightst beleeue, he causes
thee to heare the word, that thou mightst heare,
his Prophets must preach it to thee, before they
can preach, they must be sent : So that in briefe,
The Minister is sent to preach, he preaches that
thou maist heare, thou hearest, that thou mightst
be called, thou art called to beleeue in Christ,
thou beleeuest that thou maiest be iustified, being
iustified, thou art sure of thy Crowne of Glorie, and
this glory the loue of God by all these meanes sets
as it were vpon thy head.   Betweene therfore
our glory which is the end, & Gods loue which

is the beginning and cause of it, many interiacent meanes, you see, are cast betweene." (pp. 239— 241.) Again :—

(25) "If the Sunne be risen, wee shall finde him sooner by his beames vpon the tops of the Mountaines, then in the Orient of Heauen it selfe; and so the Loue of God is sooner discouered to rise in thy heart by the beames of Grace it there shows abroad, then by the flame of it self that shines in his owne breast in heauen. If then grace imbrighten thy heart, thou maist from Grace assure thy selfe of Gods loue, and thine own glorie : but if thou findest in thy selfe an impenitent and incorrigible heart, thou mayst then iustly worke vpon thy selfe a sence of thy misery : I dare not say thou art sure of Gods wrath, but I must say, except thou repent, and God change thy heart, thou art yet in a fearefull and lost estate ; say not therefore thus. God hath cast me out from his fauour, therefore my heart is obdurate, impenitent, incorrigible. For this is to argue from that thou knowest not, whether God fauors thee or no : but thus rather, My heart is obdurate, impenitent, incorrigible, therefore if I so continue, God will surely cast mee out from his fauour and presence. And this thou maist securely doe, because thine owne con-

science is both a witnesse and a iudge of thy life,
whether it be impenitent or not." (pp. 251—3.)

(26) "Nor was it a miracle to see rich mens
daughters (vnacquainted with new tires, and most
fashionable dresses) busic themselues in laborious
(and not curious needle) work, but it was ordinary
in that old world to meete the young and beautifull
Rachel tending her fathers sheepe, and watering
the flocke, and Rebecca with a pitcher vpon her
shoulder, drawing water both for her owne vse, and
to water the Camels of Abrahams servant, an
office that our nice virgins, who dresse vp themselues like so many gay silke-worms would thinke
scorne of." (pp. 262—3.)   Again:—

(27) "Thus were the opinions of the old world,
but it is a world to see now the prodigious
change of Nature, when not onelie most men count
Husbandrie a base and sordid businesse, vnfit to
soyle their hands with: but some, who thinkes his
breast tempered of finer clay then ours of the
vulgar sort, call such as haue spent their times in
the studies of Diuinity, no better then *rixosum dis-
putatorum genus quorum vix in coquendis oleribus
consilium admittit.*" (pp. 274-275).   Again:—

(28.) "Others bestow their time in Legall, and
Callings vsefull to the Common-wealth, but as they
abuse them, neyther honest, nor iustifiable before

God. Such are our Tap-houses, and Gaming Innes,
I meane not harbouring and viatory Innes, which
questionless, in fit places, and where Iustice is
neere at hand, if rightly vsed, are not onely lawfull and profitable, but necessarie and honest: for
to lodge weary Trauellers as Rahab did the Spies .
of Israel, or to let the poore labouring man to
have iust allowance of bread and drinke for his
money can be accounted no other then necessary
relief: but for our Tipling Innes in small and
vntract Hamlets, without which our Country-
Diuels of drunkennesse, Blasphemy, Gaming,
Lying, and Queaning, could amongst vs finde
no harbor (though perhaps in places of more
resort they haue credit enough to be entertained
in fairer lodgings) they are eyther the Diuels
vncleane Warehouses for his spiritual wickednesses to trade in; or in our plaine world hee hath
no traffique at all." (pp. 291-93).

(29) 'It was Eliahs speech from God to Ahab:
'Hast thou slaine, and also taken possession; and
it may well bo his Churches to either of theirs.
Hast thou taken possession, and wilt thou slay
also? not the body once, but for euer the soules,
of innocent men. Let no man quarrell with me,
as Ahab did with Eliah. 'Hast thou found me
O mine Enemie?' If he doe, I must borrow Saint

Paules answer 'Am I thine enemy, because I tell thee the Truth? No (I speake not out of rash, but charitable zeale) thou art thine owne Enimie, thou art Gods Enimie, thou art the enimie of his Church. For if thou didst loue him, thou wouldst feede his flocke, feede his Sheepe, feede his Lambs. If thou diddest loue his Church, thou wouldest shew thy loue by thy obedience to it. Who enioynes euery one eleuen moneths residence vpon his cure, and graunts him but one month's bsence, whereas it is a venture, but without long search you may finde one that absents himselfe elevuen moneths, and is resident but once a yeare, and that is perhaps at haruest, or peraduenture at Easter, when his owne, and not so much the Churchs profit calles him to his benefit, not his Benefice. He would being resident preach euery Sunday, as shee commaunds him in her 45. Cannon. Hee wonld labour to conuince Heretiques (which now in his absence growes vppon her) or see them at least censured as shee bids him in her 65. and 66. Canons. He would keepe the sound in safety, and visit the sicke, as shee directs him in her 67. Canon. Thus he would do, and not laugh at them that did thus, and would haue him doe so, as men more precise, than wise, of more heate than discretion. I am not so intemperate as to rage against all Non-residency, which in case of insüfficiencie of one Liuing, or publique, and necessarie imployment, either in Vniuersities or Court, must needs be allowable: but either our Church it selfe is precise, that bids him doe thus : or he that does the contrary without any ouer-ballancing reason, prooues himselfe a Bastard, and none of hir Children. A double wound it is our Church recciues from these men. For as them-selues haue not the grace to correct their owne sinne, so they haue commonly in their roomes certaine vnder-curats, so grossely ignorant. as not to know theirs. They that know nothing them-selues, are set by these to teach others, of whom we cannot say *dies diei*, but *nox nocti indicat scientiam.* One night teaches another, a blinde Prophet a blinde People." (pp. 397–402.) Again :—

(30) " Those Ecclesiastical home-Droanes of our owne, which hiue themselues vnder the shadow of our Church (the wicked thiefe money, that siluer dropsie, that now raigns in vnconsion-able Patrons, making way for them), and so beare indeed either no witnesse to Christ at all, or but very slight, and rash witnesse " (p. 397).

He is very severe on non-residence at page 399 *seqq* : as earlier (page 371) he had passionately

exclaimed (28) "O that there were not in Christs
militant Church, as there were in Othoes military
Campe, so many men, so few Soldiers, so many
professors, so few Christians."

That he could wield the lash effectively has
already appeared : but here is an out-burst on
contemporary literature somewhat unexpected :

(31) "Among the crowde of this ranke (idlers)
wee may thrust in our idle pamphleteers and
loose poets, no better thtn the priests of Venus,
with the rabble of stage-players, balleters and
circumferancous fidlers and brokers : all which
if they were cleane taken out of the world there
would bee little misse of them."

(32) "I do not deny but .that God is able to
perfect his power in these mens weaknesse : [The
under-curates left by non-residents]   For it is not
impossible for our spirituall Sampson (as hee ouer-
came his enemies, and was refreshed with a iawe
of the seely beast) so to make the waters of Life
spring between the teeth of these simple creatures :
but these unsent Runners might do well to content
themselues with one Cure, and not to be too busie
in trudging between many, as some of them are."
(p. 404.)

(33) "Neyther doe I denie but that such trading
Preachers may find work enough for their mouths

by making other mens labours runne through them. But this is to get their Liuing by the sweat of other men, and to wipe it off to their owne browes" (p. 405).

He then gets vulgar, abusive, and illogical:

(34) Pardon mee (right deerly beloued in our Lord and Sauiour) if when Thorns and Thistles grow vpon Gods Altar, as the Prophet Hosea speakes, I am forced to vse a little fire of Zeale to consume them." (p. 413.)

Besides these fuller specimens I have marked a number of brief ones containing unusual words and turns of expression: *e.g.*

(1) The name of the wicked 'rots'—"And therefore our Sauiour in the Storie of Lazarus, and Dives, keepes the poore mans name aliue to the worldes end, but industriously leaues the rich mans name at vncertaintie, with 'There was a certaine rich man.'" (p. 207.)

(2) "Purpled in glory by the bloud royall of our deere Lord" (p. 239.)

(3) "Those two mayne iettes......Selfe-sufficiency and Perpetuitie." (p. 121.)

(4) Seioyn'd one from another." (p. 122.)

(5) "Apting the bodies of men" (p. 269.)

(6) "Our nakednesse was then our glory, it is now our shame: it was a curse to till the earth

E

then, it is now a blessing to haue earth to till: so that wee haue learnt to turne by the corruption of our nature, our apparell that should couer our shame, to proclaime our pride : and our Lands that should feede vs by our labour, to the food of our luxurie" (pp. 277, 278)

(7) "They had need to be embalm'd as well before, as after their deaths." (p. 298)

(8) "Lessoned our reason by sence" (p. 304)

(9) "The noon-Sunne." (p. 307.)

(10) "The Christian impaths himselfe." (p. 321.)

(11) "Defalke as much from Gods word." (p. 323.)

(12) "Some of these again spanging out of the Canon of the New Testament, all the Reuelation of S John. (p. 325.)

(13) "Others farsing *into* the Canonicall writings, Apocriphall and vnknowne Authors. (p. 325.)

(14) "The strict keeping of decorum, in figuring them [the four Evangelists] like beasts ['the four Beasts') such as the Lamb himselfe is. (p. 331.)

(15) "The bulletting of a whole commonwealth." (p. 394.)

(16) "An irrepugnable truth." (p. 30.)

(17) "Were they not eftsoons reymbark't and stock't againe into the Tree of Life." (p. 43.)

(18) "The first fulnesse or saturity." (p. 50.)

(19) "Indeflowrishing and vnattainted health." (p. 51)

(20) Measured them out by God, to vessel it up in." (p. 53 and again p. 91.)

(21) "This is a retruse, and hidden, but in truth a very diuine motion" (p. 69.)

(22) "The similitude it hath with it, in the act of intellection." (p. 70.)

(23) "Inspired, and I may so speake, Spirited with the Holy Ghost." (p. 76.)

(24) "Euigilant soules." (p. 85.)

(25) "Imbondaged." (p. 107.)

I know not that I leave anything worth-while in this VOLUME: but surely you have in these words from it, 'APPLES of GOLD' in a 'BASKET of SILVER.' Biographically, our longer extracts numbered 15. and 17. are most interesting: and there are other personal touches that make the recovery of the 'Reward of the Faithfull' no common treasure-trove toward our all too scant knowledge of our Worthy.

That he was human is clear enough : infirm of temper and perchance over-vehement and over-

Churchly, and in relation to the lowly men who outside of the Church of England sought to 'speak' for the One Saviour and of the One 'Salvation' mournfully without the large charity of the illustrious JEREMY TAYLOR in his 'Liberty of Prophesying'—which may be called the 'Magna Charta' of 'Ecclesiastical History,' so potent is it still.

FULLER leaves the death-date of our Poet imperfect thus 162.. but ANTHONY A-WOOD supplies it, viz., 1623.* "I beheld," says the former, "the life of this learned poet, like those half-verses in Virgil's Æneid, broken off in the middle, seeing he might have doubled his days according to the ordinary course of nature."‡ That 1623 was our Worthy's death-year is con- firmed inferentially by PHINEAS's over-looked verses headed "Upon my brother's book called, The grounds, labour and reward of faith," than which nothing can more meetly close our Intro- duction :

> " This lamp fill'd up, and fir'd by that blest Spirit
> Spent his last oyl in this pure, heav'nly flame ;
> Laying the grounds, walls, roof of faith : this frame
> *With life he ends ;* and now doth there inherit

---

* As before, *s. n.*   † As before : 'Worthies' *s. n.*

What here he built, crown'd with his laurel merit :
  Whose palms and triumphs once he loudly rang,
  There now enjoyes what here he sweetly sang.
This is his monument, on which he drew
His spirit's image, that can never die ;
But breathes in these live words, and speaks to th' eye :
In these his winding-sheets he dead doth shew
To buried souls the way to live anew,
  And in his grave more powerfully now preacheth :
  Who will not learn, when that a dead man teacheth ?"*

No stone,—and so no 'golden lie' of epitaph—or any other outward memorial whatever, marks GILES FLETCHER's last resting-place. He left a Widow—as we have already seen—who transferred herself to another and neighbouring Rectory. Who she was, and whether she bore a family to her first husband, has not been ' written.'

In our edition of the complete ' Poems ' of PHINEAS FLETCHER, I hope to furnish an Essay on the Poetry of the two Brothers, and therein to bring out their characteristics, and their influence, on MILTON and others; and also to present critical judgments on both, from various sources—satisfied that GILES and PHINEAS FLETCHER need only to be known to secure a very much more adequate

---

* Poeticall Miscellanies, pp. 101, 102 (1663).

recognition than has yet been accorded; and
equally so, that otherwise well-read and cultured
men are deplorably ignorant of these and other
of our ancient 'Makkars.'

And so the little life-story is told of one, con-
cerning whom loveable old LIVESEY's eulogium of
CHETHAM, holds, "They who excell[ed] him in
grace, came short of him in learning: and they
who excell'd him in learning came short of him
in grace."* Turning then to his noble Poem

> "Now his faith, his works, his ways,
> Nights of watching, toilsome days,
> Borne for Christ, 'tis meet we praise."

ALEXANDER B. GROSART.

15 ST. ALBAN'S PLACE,
    BLACKBURN, LANCASHIRE.

P.S. With reference to our Poet's presentation
to ALDERTON (see page 25 *ante*), Mr. Wright of
Cambridge (as before) has kindly sent me the
following note: "In Bacon's *Liber Regis* edn.
1786, p. 782, under the head of Alderton I find
' Sir James Bacon pro duabus vicibus, olim Patr.'

---

* 'Greatest Loss,' page 9.

Is it not probable that the living was in the gift of the Bacon Family in Fletcher's time, and that even Sir Francis Bacon may have presented him to it?" This confirms my question *in loco*: and it is very disappointing that the Alderton 'Registers' and other Manuscripts have been allowed to waste and perish. G.

EPISTLE DEDICATORY.

TO the Right Worshipvll [sic], and Reverend Mr. Doctour Nevile, Deane of Canterbvrie, and the Master of Trinitie Colledge in Cambridge.*

Right worthie, and reverend Syr:

As I haue alwaies thought the place wherein I liue, after heauen, principally to bee desired, both because I most want and it most abounds with wisdome, which is fled by some with as much delight, as it is obtained by others, and ought to be followed by all: so I cannot but next unto God, for euer acknowledge myselfe most bound vnto the hand of God, (I meane yourselfe) that reacht downe, as it were out of heauen, vnto me, a benefit of that nature and price, then which, I could wish none, (onely heauen itselfe excepted) her more fruitfull, and contenting for the time it

---

* For notice of Dean NEVILLE see TODD's 'Account of the Deans of Canterbury.' He died May 2, 1615.   G.

that is now present, or more comfortable, and en-couraging for the time that is alreadie past, or more hopefull, and promising for the the time that is yet to come.

For as in all mens iudgements (that haue any iudgement) Europe is worthily deem'd the Queene of the world, that Garland both of Learning, and pure Religion beeing now become her crowne, and blossoming vpon her head, that hath long since laine withered in Greece and Palestine; so my opinion of this Island hath alwaies beene, that it is the very face, and beautie of all Europe, in which both true Religion is faithfully pro-fessed without superstition, and (if on earth) true Learning sweetly flourishes without ostentation: and what are the twoo eyes of this Land, but the two Vniversities; which cannot but prosper in the time of such a Prince, that is a Prince of Learning as well as of People :* and truly I should forget myselfe, if I should not call Cambrigge the right eye: and I thinke (King Henrie the 8. beeing the vniter, Edward the 3. the Founder, and your selfe the Repairer of this Colledge, wherein I liue) none will blame me, if I esteeme the same, since

---

* James I. G.

your polishing of it, the fairest sight in Cambridge :
in which beeing placed by your onely fauour, most
freely, without either any meanes from other, or
any desert in my selfe, beeing not able to doe more,
I could doe no lesse, then acknowledge that debt,
which I shall neuer be able to pay, and with
old Silenus, in the Poet (vpon whome the boyes—
*injiciunt ipsis ex vincula sertis** making his garland,
his fetters) finding my selfe bound vnto you by so
many benefits, that were giuen by your selfe for
ornaments, but are to me as so many golden
chcines, to hold me fast in a kind of desired bondage,
seeke (as he doth) my freedome with a song, the
matter whereof is as worthie the sweetest
Singer, as my selfe, the miserable Singer, vnworthie
so diuine a subiect : but the same fauour, that
before rewarded no desert, knowes now as well
how to pardon all faults, then which indulgence,
when I regard my selfe, I can wish no more;
when I remember you, I can hope no lesse.

So commending these few broken lines vnto
yours, and your selfe into the hands of the best
physitian, Iesvs Christ, with whome, the most
ill affected man in the midst of his sicknes, is in

---

* Virgil Ecl. vi. 19.   G.

good health, and without whome, the most lustie
bodie, in his greatest iollitie, is but a languishing
karease, I humbly take my leaue, ending with the
same wish, that your deuoted Observer, and my
approoued Friend doth, in his verses presently
sequent, that your passage to heauen may be
slow to vs, that shall want you here, but to your
selfe, that cannot want vs there, most secure and
certeyne.

Your Worships, in all dutie, and seruice

G. FLETCHER.

THOMAS NEVYLE.
MOST HEAVENLY.

As when the Captaine of the heauenly host,
Or else that glorious armie doth appeare
In waters drown'd, with surging billowes tost,
We know they are not, where we see they are ;
　　We see them in the deepe, we see them mooue,
　　We know they fixed are in heauen aboue :

So did the Sunne of righteousnesse come downe
Clowded in flesh, and seem'd be in the deepe :
So doe the many waters seeme to drowne
The starres his Saints, and they on earth to keepe,
　　And yet this Sunne from heauen neuer fell,
　　And yet these earthly starres in heauen dwell.

What if their soules be into prison cast
In earthly bodies ? yet they long for heauen ;
What if this worldly Sea they haue not past ?
Yet faine they would be brought into their hauen.
　　They are not here, and yet we here them see,
　　For euery man is there, where he would be.

Long may you wish , and yet long wish in vaine,
Hence to depart, and yet that wish obtaine.
Long may you here in heauen on earth remaine,
And yet a heauen in heauen hereafter gaine.
　　Go you to heauen, but yet O make no hast,
　　Go slowly slowly, but yet go at last.
　　　　But when the Nightingale so neere doth sit,
　　　　Slence the Titmouse better may befit.

F. NETHERSOLE.

TO THE READER.

THEAR are but fewe of many that can rightly iudge of Poetry; and yet thear ar many of those few, that carry so left-handed an opinion of it, as some of them thinke it halfe sacrilege for prophane Poetrie to deale with divine and heauenly matters, as though David wear to be sentenced by them, for vttering his graue matter vpon the harpe : others something more violent in their censure, but sure lesse reasonable (as though Poetrie corrupted all good witts, when, indeed, bad witts corrupt Poetrie) banish it with Plato out of all well-ordered Commonwealths. Both theas I will striue rather to satisfie, then refute.

And of the first I would gladlie knowe, whither they suppose it fitter, that the sacred songs in the Scripture of those heroicall Saincts, Moses, Deborah, Ieremie, Mary, Simeon, Dauid, Salomon (the wisest Scholeman, and wittiest Poet) should bee eiected from the canon, for wante of grauitie, or

rather this erroure eraced out of their mindes, for
wante of truth. But, it maye bee, they will giue
the Spirit of God leaue to breath through what
pipe it please, & will confesse, because they
must needs, that all the songs dittied by him,
must needs bee, as their Fountaine is, most holy :
but their common clamour is, who may compare
with God ? true; & yet as none may compare
without presumption, so all may imitat, and not
without commendation : which made Nazianzen,
on[e] of the Starrs of the Greeke Church, that
nowe shines as bright in heauen, as he did then
on earth, write so manie diuine Poems of the
Genealogie, Miracles, Parables, Passion of Christ,
called by him his χριστὸς πάσχων * : which when
Basil, the Prince of the Fathers, and his Chamber
fellowe, had seene, his opinion of them was, that
he could haue deuised nothing either more fruitfull
to others—because it kindly woed them to
Religion, or more honourable to himselfe οὐδὲν γὰρ
μακαριώτερον ἐστι τοῦ τὴν ἀγγέλων χορείαν ἐν γῇ μι-
μεῖσθαι, because by imitating the singing Angels in
heaun, himselfe became, though before his time, an

---

* The Cento called *Christus Patiens* is printed in his
Works, Vol. II., 253 (Paris 1636).   G.

earthly Angel.* What should I speake of Iuven-
cus, Prosper, and wise Prudentius? the last of
which, liuing in Hieroms time, twelue hundred
yeares agoe, brought foorth in his declining age,
so many, & so religious poems, straitly charging
his soule, not to let passe so much as one either
night or daye without some diuine song, *Hymnis*
continuet dies, Nec nox ulla vacet, quin Dominum
canat.† And as sedulous Prudentius, so prudent
Sedulius was famous in this poeticall diuinity,
tho coetan‡ of Bernard, who sung the historie of
Christ with as much deuotion in himself, as
admiration to others; all which wear followed by
the choicest witts of Christendome; Nonnius
translating all Sainct Iohns Ghostpel into Greek
verse, Sanazar, the late-liuing Image, and happy
imitator of Virgil, bestowing ten yeares vpon a
song, onely to celebrat that one day when Christ
was borne vnto vs on earth, & we (a happie
change) vnto God in heau'n: thrice-honour'd
Bartas, & our (I know no other name more
glorious then his own) Mr. Edmund Spencer (two
blessed Soules) not thinking ten years inough,

---

* Epist. ad Gregorium Theolog. 1. G.
† Prudentius, Cathemerinon liber, præf. 37, 38. G.
‡ Contemporary. G.

layeing out their whole liues vpon this one studie :
Nay I may iustly say, that the Princely Father of
our Countrey (though in my conscience, God hath
made him of all the learned Princes that euer
wear the most religious, and of all the religious
Princes, the most learned, that so, by the one, hee
might oppose him against the Pope, the peste of
of all Religion and by the other, against Bellar-
mine the abuser of all good Learning) is yet so far
enamour'd with this celestiall Muse, that it shall
neuer repent mee—*calamo triuisse labellum*, when-
socuer I shall remember *Hæc eadem ut sciret quid
non faciebat Amyntas ?*[*] To name no more in such
plenty, whear I may finde how to beginne,
sooner then to end, Saincte Paule, by the
Example of Christ, that wente singing to mounte
Oliuet, with his Disciples, after his last supper,
exciteth the Christians to solace themselues with
hymnes, and Psalmes, and spirituall songs; and
thearefore by their leav's, be it an error for Poets
to be Divines, I had rather err with the Scripture,
then be rectifi'd by them : I had rather adore the
stepps of Nazianzen, Prudentius, Sedulius, then
followe their steps, to bee misguided : I had rather

---

* Virgil, Ecl. ii., 34, 35. G.

be the deuoute Admirer of Nonnius, Bartas, my
sacred Soueraign, and others, the miracles of our
latter age, then the false sectarie of these, that
haue nothing at all to follow, but their own naked
opinions: To conclude, I had rather with my
Lord, and his most divine Apostle sing (though I
sing sorilie) the loue of heauen and earthe, then
praise God (as they doe) with the woorthie guift
of silence, and sitting still, or think I dispraisd
him with this poetical discourse. It seems they
haue either not read, or clean forgot, that it is the
dutie of the Muses (if wee may beeleeue Pindare,
and Hesiod) to sit allwaies vnder the throne of
Iupiter, *eius et laudes et beneficia* 'υμνειουσας which
made a very worthy German writer conclude
it *Certò statuimus, proprium atque: peculiare
poetarium munus esse, Christi gloriam illustrare*
beeing good reason that the heauenly infusion of
such Poetry. shouldende in his glorie, that had
beginning from his goodnes, *fit orator, nascitur
Poeta.*

For the secound sorte thearfore, that eliminat
Poets out of their citie gates; as though they
wear nowe grown so bad, as they could neither
growe woorse, nor better though it be somewhat
hard for those to bee the onely men should want
cities, that wear the onely causers of the building

F

of them and somewhat inhumane to thrust them
into the woods, to liue among the beasts, who
wear the first that call'd men out of the woods,
from their beastly, and wilde life, yet since they will
needes shoulder them out for the onely firebrands
to inflame lust (the fault of earthly men, not
heauenly Poetrie) I would gladly learne, what
kind of professions theas men would bee intreated
to entertaine, that so deride and disaffect Poesie :
would they admit of Philosophers, that after they
haue burnt out the whole candle of their life in
the circular studie of Sciences, crie out at length,
Se nihil prorsus scire? or should Musitians be welcome to them, that. *Dant sine mente sonum*—bring
delight with them indeede, could they aswell
expresse with their instruments a voice, as they
can a sound? or would they most approve of
Soldiers that defend the life of their countrymen
either by the death of themselues, or their enemies ?
If Philosophers please them, who is it, that knowes
not, that all the lights of Example, to cleare their
precepts, are borrowed by Philosophers from Poets;
that without Homers examples, Aristotle would
be as blind as Homer : If they retaine Musitians,
who euer doubted, but that Poets infused the verie
soule into the inarticulate sounds of musique ; that
without Pindar & Horace the Lyriques had beene

silenced for euer: If they must needes entertaine
Soldiers, who can but confesse, that Poets restore
againe that life to soldiers, which they before lost
for the safetie of their country; that without
Virgil, Æneas had neuer beene so much as heard
of. How then can they for shame deny commonwealths to them, who weare the first Authors of
them; how can they denie the blinde Philosopher,
that teaches them, his light; the emptie Musitian
that delights them, his soule; the dying Soldier,
that defends their life, immortalitie, after his owne
death; let Philosophie, let Ethiques, let all the
Arts bestowe vpon vs this guift, that we be not
thought dead men, whilest we remaine among the
liuing: it is onely Poetrie that can make vs be
thought liuing men, when we lie among the dead,
and therefore I thinke it vnequall to thrust them
out of our cities, that call vs out of our graues,
to thinke so hardly of them, that make vs to be
so well thought of to deny them to liue a while
among vs, that make vs liue for euer among our
Posteritie.

So beeing nowe weary in perswading those that
hate, I commend my selfe to those that loue such
Poets, as Plato speakes of, that sing diuine and
heroical matters, οὐ γὰρ οὗτοι εἰσὶν, ὃι ταῦτα

λέγοντες, ἀλλ ὁ Θεὸς, αὐτός ἐστιν ὁ λέγων,* recommending theas my idle howers, not idly spent, to good schollers, and good Christians, that haue ouercome their ignorance with reason, and their reason, with religion.

---

* Plato *Ion.* p. 181. D : G.

PRELIMINARY VERSES.

Fond ladds that spend so fast your poasting time,
('Too poasting time, that spends your time as fast)
To chaunt light toyes, or frame some wanton rime,
Where idle boyes may glut their lustful tast;
Or else with praise to cloath some fleshly slime
With virgins roses and faire lillies chast;
   While itching bloods and youthfull eares adore it;
But wiser men, and once yourselues, will most
    abhorre it.

But thou (most neere, most deare) in this of thine
Hast proov'd the Muses not to Venus bound;
Such as thy matter, such thy Muse, divine;
Or thou such grace with Merci's self tast found,
That she herself deign's in thy leaues to shine;
Or stol'n from heav'n, thou brought'st this verse to
    ground,
   Which frights the nummèd soule with fearfull thunder,
And soone with honied dewes melts it 'twixt ioy and
    wonder.

Then doe not thou malitious tongnes esteeme ;
The glasse, through which an envious eye doth gaze,
Can easily make a mo̧le-hill mountaines seeme
His praise dispraises, his dispraises praise ;
Enongh, if best men best thy labours deem,
And to the highest pitch thy merit raise ;
  While all the Muses to thy song decree
Victorious Triumph, triumphant Victorie.

PHIN. FLETCHER, Regal.

    Quid ô, quid Veneres, Cupidinesq,
    Turturesq., iocosq., passcresq
    Lascivi canitis greges, poëtæ ?
    Et iam languidulos amantum ocellos,
    Et mox turguidulas sinu papillas,
    Iam risus * teneros, lachrymulasq., †
    Mox suspiria, morsiunculasq.,
    Mille basia ; mille, mille nugas ?
    Et vultus pueri, puellululæve
    (Heu fusci pueri, puellulæq.)
    Pingitis nivibus, rosunculisq.,
    (Mentitis nivibus, rosunculisq.)
    Quæ vel primo hyemis rigore torpent,
    Vel Phœbi intuitu statim relanguent ?
    Heu stulti nimiùm greges poetæ !
    Vt, quas sic nimis, ah nimis stupetis,
    (Nives candidulæ & rosæ pudentes)
    Sic vobis pereunt statim labores :

---

       * 'Fletus' 1632 edn. G.
       † 'Cachinnulosque' *ib.* G.

Et solem fugiunt severiorem,
Vel saltem gelida rigent senectâ :
   At tu qui clypeo, haud inane nomen
   (Minervæ clypeo Iovisq.) sumens
Victrices resonas Dei Triumphos,
Triumphos lacbrymis, metuq. plenos,
   Plenos lætitiæ, & spei triumphos,
   Dum rem carmine, Pieroq. dignam
Aggrederis, tibi res decora rebus
Præbet carmina, Pieroq. digna.
Quin ille ipse tuos legens triumphos,
Plenos militia, labore plenos ;
   Tuo propitius parat labori
   Plenos lætitiæ & spei triumphos.

PHIN. FLETCHER, Regal.

'Η Μαριὰμ

Μὴ μιαρὰ.

Beatissima virginum Maria,
Sed materq. simul beata, per quam
Qui semper fuit ille cœpit esse :
Quæ Vitæ dederisq. inire vitam :
Et Luci dediris videre lucem :
   Quæ fastidia, morsiunculásq.
Passa es quas grauidæ solent, nec unquam
Audebas propior viro venire,
Dum clusus * penetralibus latebat

---

* 'Clausus' ib.   G

Matricis tunicâ undiq. involutus,
Quem se posse negant tenere cœli.
Quæ non virgineas premi papillas
Passa, virgineas tamen dedisti
Lactandas puero tuo papillas.
Eia, dic age, dic beata virgo,
Cur piam abstineas manum timesq.
Sancta tangere, Sanctuariumq :
Insolens fugias ? an inquinari
Contactu metuis tuo sacrata ?
Contactu metuit suo sacrata
Pollui pia, cernis en ferentem,
Lenimenta Dei furentis, illa
Fædatas sibi ferre quæ iubebat.
Sis felix noua virgo-mater opto,
Quæ mollire Deum paras amicum.
Quin hîc dona licet licet relinquas,
Agnellumq. repone, turturemq..
Audax ingrediare inanis ædes
Dei, tange Deo sacrata, tange.
Quæ non concubitu coinquinata,
Agnellum peperitq,   Turturemq,
Exclusit, facili Deo litabit
Agno cum Deus insit, & columbæ.

Nor can I so much say as much I ought,
Nor yet so little can I say as nought,
In praise of this thy worke, so heauenly pend,
That sure the sacred Dove a quill did lend
From her high-soaring wing : certes I know
No other plumes, that makes man seeme so low

In his owne eyes, who to all others sight
Is mounted to the highest pitch of height:
Where if thou seeme to any of small price,
The fault is not in thee, but in his eyes:
But what doe I thy flood of wit restreine
Within the narrow bankes of my poore veyne?
More I could say, and would, but that to praise
Thy verses, is to keepe them from their praise.
For them who reades, and doth them not aduance,
Of envie doth it, or of ignorance.

F. NETHERSOLE.*

In 1632 edition there is added here a couplet:

Defuncto fratri,

Think (if thou cans't) how mounted on his spheare
In heaven now he sings: thus sung he here.

PHIN. FLETCHER. Regal.   G.

---

* NETHERSOLE was 'Public Orator' of the University
(of Cambridge), in which office he was succeeded by
GEORGE HERBERT, who, like GILES FLETCHER, was a
protege of Dean Nevile.   Lowndes 'calls him Sir
Francis as author of a forgotten Latin tractate (See
s. n.)   Nethersole fell under the scorpion lash of
JOHN GOODWIN, who had been assailed by him very
grossly and unrighteously.   G.

CHRIST'S
VICTORIE AND TRIUMPH.

NOTE.

THE original title-page, as well as those of the second and third editions, will be found annexed: also collation of each edition. The changes from the first (1610) are wholly modernisation of the spelling. Our text is that of 1610; to the orthography of which, throughout, we adhere strictly—save that the usual mark of apostrophe of the possessive case is inserted e. g. Rome's not Romes, and that the capitals and italics are occasionally diminished and occasionally encreased—the latter in the Divine names—nouns and pronouns—and in Impersonations. The punctuation is also accommodated to modern usage: the original consists mainly of a profusion of commas. As the Poet was dead before the second edition appeared, the text of 1610 is the only one that bears his authority. Exemplifications of the faulty character of re-prints hitherto, will be found in the foot-notes, where the most flagrant mis-prints, etc., etc., of three of the best

arc given viz. (1) RICHARDSON's: "Christ's Victory
and Triumph in Heaven and Earth, over and after
Death, in Four Parts. By Giles Fletcher. With
an Original Biographical Sketch of the Author,
&c. Also some Choice Pieces from the Poetical
Writings of the Rev. George Herbert, Late Orator
of the University of Cambridge. London :
Published by T. Richardson, 98, High Holborn,
and B. Clark. 1824. cr. 8vo. pp. xiv. and pp.
130." This is a somewhat ambitions but a very
poor edition. There is nothing 'original' in the
'Biographical Sketch' except that while adding
nothing to former scanty materials it contrives to
multiply 'blunders' The orthography is modernized throughout and the sense repeatedly mistaken. Probably the Publisher—who was also
the Printer—was his own Editor. I designate
it by Richardson : but he is not to be confounded
with DR. RICHARDSON, to whom we have frequent occasion to refer in our notes. (2) Sou-
THEY's: in his 'British Poets: Chaucer to Jonson.'
(1831, 8vo.) He disclaims responsibility for the
proof-sheets : but he must be held responsible
for the selection of his texts. (3) CATTERMOLE's :
in his "Sacred Poetry of the 17th Century."
(1836, 2 vols. 12mo.) both modernized and
carelessly read. I have not deemed it worth-

while to add the like mis-prints and corruptions
of the general collations of what are called ' The
Poets ' by Dr. Anderson and by Chalmers. That
of 1783 (8vo) along with 'The Purple Island' is
beneath criticism. Throughout I have added
foot-notes as required—passing over trite classical
allusions and names. I have very heartily to
acknowledge the scholarly aid of my friend W.
ALDIS WRIGHT, Esq., M.A., of Trinity College,
Cambridge, in verifying and correcting such
allusions and quotations as I found any difficulty
with. He has rendered me careful and ungrudging help in all my labours on these
Poets. G.

(*a*)   1st edition:

CHRISTS

VICTORIE, AND TRI-

umph in Heauen, and Earth,

over, and after death.

———

A te principium, tibi desinet, accipe iussis
Carmina cæpta tuis, atque hanc sine tempora circum
Inter victrices hederam tibi scrpere lauros.

———

Cambridge
Printed by C. Legge.   1610.   [small 4to.]

Collation: Title-page—Epistle Dedicatory pp. 3—
Nethersole's ' Verses ' 1 page—to the Reader pp. 5—
Phin. Fletcher's and Nethersole's ' Verses ' pp. 4—[un-
[unpaged]—Poem pp. 83 and Latin ' Lines ' 1 page.
Opposite blank reverse of page 45 is a separate title-page
' Christ's Trivmph ouer and after Death.   Vincenti
dabitur.   Printed by C. Legge, 1610.   After page 79 by
an oversight mispages 81 and so runs—

(*b*) 2nd edition:

CHRISTS

VICTORIE AND

TRIUMPH IN HEAVEN

AND EARTH, OVER

AND AFTER DEATH.

———

A te principium, tibi dosinet: accepe jussis
Carmina cœpta tuis, atq hanc sine tempora circum
Inter victrices hederam tibi serpere lauros.

———

The second Edition.

———

Cambridge:
Printed for Francis Green. 1632. [Small 4to]

Collation: Title-page—Epistle Dedicatory pp. 3—
Nethersole's 'Verses' 1 page—to the Reader pp. 4—
Phin. Fletcher's and Netersole's 'Verses' pp. 4—
[unpaged]—Poem pp. 83 and Latin 'Lines' on page 84.
Opposite page '42 is the separate title as *supra* 'Christ's
Triumph ouer and after Death. Vincenti dabitur. Printed
by the Printers to the Universitie of Cambridge. Ann.
Dom. 1632.'

ı

(*c*)   3rd edition.

CHRISTS

VICTORY

AND

TRIVMPH.

In *Heaven* and *Earth*, over and after

Death.

Wherein is } His { Birth.
lively figured   *Circumcision.*
                             Baptism.
                             Temptation.
                             Passion.
                             Resurrection.
                             Ascention.

In foure divine Poems.

———

Cambridge :

Printed by *Roger Daniel*, for *Richard Royston*.   1640.

[Small 4to.[

Collation : same as 2nd edition : and seven engravings
as described in our Appendix to the Poem. The above
separate title not in 3rd edition.   **G.**

CONTENTS.

CHRIST'S
VICTORIE AND TRIUMPH.

THE ARGUMENT.*

The Argument propounded in generall: Our redemption by Christ:
st. 1, 2.—The Author's inuocation for the better handling of it:
st. 3, 4.—The Argument [in its details G.]: Man's redemption
expounded from the cause—Mercie dwelling in heauen, and plead-
ing for man now guiltie, with Justice described by her qualities:
st. 5—11. Her retinue: st. 12—14.—Her subiects: st. 15, 16.—Her
accusation of man's sinne: st. 17. And (I.) of Adam's first sinne:
st. 18, 19.—Then of his posteritie's, in all kinde of idolatrie: st. 20
—24. How hopelesse any patronage of it: st. 25—27.—All the
creatures hauing disleagued themselues with him for his extreame
ungratefulnes: st. 28—34.—So that beeng destitute of all hope or
any remedie, he can look for nothing but a fearful sentence: st. 35
—39.—The effect of Justice, her speech: the inflammation of the
heauenly powers appeased by Mercie, who is described by her
cherfulnes to defend man: st. 40—42.—Our inabilitie to describe
her: st. 43, 44.—Her beautie resembled by the creatures, which are
all fraile shadows of her essentiall perfection: st. 45, 46.—Her
attendants: st. 46, 47.—Her persuasiue power: st. 48—50.—Her
kind offices to man: st. 51, 52.—Her garments, wrought by her
owne hands, wherewith shee cloaths herselfe, composd of all the
creatures: st. 53.—The Earth: st. 54.—Sea; st. 55, 56.—Ayre: st. 57,
58.—The celestiall bodies: st. 59, 60.—The third heauen: st. 61, 62.
—Her obiects: st. 63.—Repentance: st. 64—66.—Faith: st. 67—69.
—Her deprecative spech for man; in which she translates the
principal fault vnto the deuill; and, repeating Justice her aggra-
vation of man's sinne, mitigates it. (1) By a contrarie inference:
(2) By interessing[1] her selfe in the cause, and[Christ: st. 70—75.—
that is as sufficient to satisfie, as man was impotent: st. 76, 77.—
Whom shee celebrates from the time of his natiuitie: st. 78. From
the effects of it in himselfe: st. 79, 80.—Egypt: st. 81.—The angels
[and] men: st. 82, 83.—The effect of Mercie's speech: st. 84.—A
transition to Christ's second victorie: st. 85.

---

* In the author's own edition and in those of 1632 and
  1640, 'The Argument' is dispersed over the margins
  opposite the several stanzas. It has been thought
  better to bring it together at the commencement of
  each Part. G.

1. Richardson, Southey, and Cattermole, misprint 'inter-
  cessing'=interceding: Fletcher himself as *supra*. G.

CHRIST'S VICTORIE IN HEAVEN.

1.

THE birth of Him that no beginning knewe,
Yet giues beginning to all that are borne;
And how the Infinite farre greater grewe,
By growing lesse, and how the rising Morne,
That shot from heau'n, did¹ backe to heau'n
     retourne;
  The obsequies of Him that could not die,
  And death of life, ende of eternitie,
How worthily He died, that died vnworthily;—

2.

How God and Man did both embrace each other,
Met in one person, Heau'n and Earth did kiss;
And how a virgin did become a mother,
And bare that Sonne, Who the world's father is,
And maker of His mother; and how bliss
  Descended from the bosome of the High,

To cloath Himselfe in naked miserie,
Sayling at length to Heau'n, in Earth, triumph-
   antly—[1]

3.

Is the first flame, wherewith my whiter Muse
Doth burne in heauenly loue, such loue to tell.
O Thou that didst this holy fire infuse,
And taught'st this brest—but late the graue of hell,
Wherein a blind and dead heart liu'd—to swell
   With better thoughts, send downe those lights
     that lend
   Knowledge, how to begin, and how to end
The loue, that neuer was, nor euer can be pend.[2]

4.

Ye Sacred Writings, in whose antique leaues
The memories of Heau'n entreasur'd lie,
Say, what might be the cause that Mercie heaues
The dust of sinne aboue th' industrious skie,

---

1. I may be allowed to refer to my "Lord Bacon not the
   Author of 'The Christian Paradoxes,' being a re-print
   of Memorials of Godliness and Christianity, by
   Herbert Palmer, B.D. With Introduction, Memoir
   and Notes." 8vo., 1865. Probably Palmer had the
   'Paradoxes' suggested by Fletcher. G.
2. 'Penned'=written or described: but cf. stanza 17,
   line 7 =confined. G

And lets it not to dust and ashes flie?
  Could Justice be of sinne so ouer-wooed,
  Or so great ill be cause of so great good,
That bloody man to saue, man's Sauiour shed His
    blood?

5.

Or did the lips of Mercie droppe soft speech
For traytrous man, when at th' Eternall's throne
Incensèd Nemesis[1] did Heau'n beseech
With thundring voice, that Iustice might be showne
Against the rebells, that from God were flowne?
  O say, say how could Mercie plead for those
  That, scarcely made, against their Maker rose?
Will any slay his friend that he may spare his
    foes?

6.

There is a place beyond that flaming hill,
From whence the starres their thin apparence shed;
A place, beyond all place, where neuer ill,
Nor impure thought, was euer harbourèd,
But sainctly heroes are for euer s'ed[2]

1.=Personification of Conscience. Cf. Hesiod, Theog.
  223. G.
2. Southey 'su'd:' Cattermole 'said:' Query=saved? G.

To keepe an euerlasting Sabbaoth's rest,
Still wishing that, of what th' ar still possest,
Enioying but oue ioy,—but one of all ioyes best.

Here, when the ruine of that beauteous frame,
Whose golden buildlng shin'd with euerie starre
Of excellence, deform'd with age became,
Mercy, remembring peace in midst of warre,
Lift vp the musique of her voice, to barre
    Eternall Fate, least it should quite erace
    That from the world, which was the first world's
      grace,
And all againe into their nothing—Chaos—chase.

8

For what had all this All which man in one
Did not vnite? the earth, aire, water, fire,
Life, sense, and spirit, nay, the powreful throne
Of the diuinest Essence, did retire,
And His owne image into clay inspire:
    So that this creature well might called be
    Of the great world the small epitomie,
Of the dead world, the liue and quicke[1] anatomie.

---

1. Living, alive, as Shakespere, (Hamlet v. 1.) "'Tis
    for the dead, not for the quick." Cf. Numbers xvi.
    30. G.

explicatul (mergey) mugue tus

9.

But Iustice had no sooner Mercy seene
Smoothing the wrinkles of her Father's browe,
But vp she starts, and throwes herself betweene :
As when a vapour, from a moory slough,
Meeting with fresh Eoüs,[1] that but now
   Open'd the world, which all in darknesse lay,
   Doth heau'ns bright face of his rayes disaray,
And sads the smiling Orient of the springing day.

10.

She was a Virgin of austere regard ;
Not as the world esteemes her, deafe and blind ;
But as the eagle, that hath oft compar'd
Her eye with Heau'n's, so, and more brightly
     shin'd
Her lamping sight; for she the same could winde
   Into the solid heart, and with her eares
   The silence of the thought loude speaking heares,
And in one hand a paire of euen scoals[2] she weares. C

11.

No riot of affection reuell kept
Within her brest, but a still apathy

---

1 Eos: in Latin, Aurora, the goddess of tho Morning who
  brings up the light of Day from the East. Cf. Hesiod.
  Theog. 371 &c. G.
2 Scales. G.

Possessèd all her soule, which softly slept
Securely, without tempest; no sad crie
Awakes her pittie, but wrong'd pouertie,
    Sending her eyes to heau'n swimming in teares,
    With hideous clamours euer struck her eares,
Whetting the blazing sword, that in her hand she
    beares.

12.

The winged Lightning is her Mercury,
And round about her mightie thunders sound:
Impatient of himselfe lies pining by
Pale Sicknes with his kercher'd[1] head vpwound,
And thousand noysome plagues attend her round;
    But if her clowdie browe but once grow foule,
    The flints doe melt, and rocks to water rowle,
And ayrie mountaines shake, and frighted shadowes
    howle.

13.

Famine, and bloodles Care, and bloodie Warre,
Want, and the want of knowledge how to vse
Abundance, Age, and Feare, that runnes afarre
Before his fellowe Greefe, that aye pursues

---

1 Milton has 'Chercheft' in Il Penseroso 125 'But Cher-
chef't in a comely Cloud' G.

His winged steps ; for who would not refuse
  Greefe's companie, a dull and rawebon'd spright,
  That lankes the cheekes, and pales the freshest
    sight,
Vnbosoming the cheereful brest of all delight.

14.

Before this cursed throng, goes Ignorance,
That needes will leade the way he cannot see :
And, after all, Death doeth his flag aduance,
And, in the midst, Strife still would roaguing[1] be,
Whose ragged flesh and cloaths did well agree :
  And round about amazed Horror flies,
  And ouer all, Shame veiles his guiltie eyes,
And vnderneath, Hell's hungrie throat still yawning
  lies.

15.

Vpon two stonie tables, spread before her,
She lean'd her bosome, more then stonie hard ;
There slept th' vnpartiall Iudge, and strict restorer
Of wrong or right, with paine or with reward ;
There hung the skore of all our debts, the card
  Whear good, and bad, and life, and death were
    painted :

---

1 Raging. G.

Was neuer heart of mortall so vntainted,
But when that scroule was read, with thousand
    terrors fainted.

16.

Witnes the thunder that mount Sinai heard,
When all the hill with firie clouds did flame,
And wandring Israel with the sight afeard,
Blinded with seeing, durst not touch the same,
But like a wood of shaking leaues became.
  On this dread[1] Justice, she, the Liuing Lawe
  Bowing herselfe with a majestique awe,
All heau'n, to heare her speech, did into silence
    drawe.

17.

' Dread Lord of spirits, well Thou did'st deuise
To fling the world's rude dunghill, and the drosse
Of the ould Chaos, farthest from the skies,
And thine Owne seate, that heare[2] the childe of
    losse
Of all the lower heau'n, the curse and crosse,
  That wretch, beast, caytiue monster—Man,
    might spend,
  (Proude of the mire in which his soule is pend)
Clodded in lumps of clay, his wearie life to end.

---

1 Misprinted by Fletcher himself 'dead.' G.
2 Richardson has 'hear', Cattermole misprints 'there' G.

18.

His bodie dust: whear growe such cause of
    pride ?
His soule Thy image : what could he enuie ?
Himselfe most happie : if he so would bide,
Now grow'n most wretched, who can remedie ?
He slewe himselfe, himselfe the enemie.
    That his owne soule would, her owne murder
      wreake :
If I were silent, Heau'n and Earth would speake
And, if all fayl'd, these stones would into clamours
    breake.

19

' How many darts made furrowes in his side,
When she, that out of his owne side was made
Gaue feathers to their flight[1] ? where was the pride
Of their newe knowledge? whither did it fade,
When, running from Thy voice into the shade,
    He fled Thy sight, himselfe of sight bereaued ;

---

1 Cf. Æschylus, Myrmidones, frag. Bp. Butler in his
note on this fragt, quotes Waller's sonnet commencing
'That Eagle's fate, &c. Byron applies it pathetically
to Kirk White. See a learned discussion of the whole
question, by Gataker, Advers. Misc. Posth. cap. XII. G.

And for his shield a leauie armour weau'd,
With which, vain man, he thought God's eies to
   haue deceaud[1] ?

20.

' And well he might delude those eyes, that see,
And iudge by colours : for who euer sawe
A man of leaues, a reasonable tree ?
But those that from this stocke their life did drawe,
Soone made their father godly, and by lawe
  Proclaimed trees almightie : gods of wood,
Of stocks, and stones with crownes of laurell stood
Templed, and fed by fathers with their childrens'
   blood.

21.

' The sparkling fanes, that burne in beaten gould,
And, like the starres of heau'n in mid'st of night
Blacke Egypt, as her mirrhours doth behould,
Are but the denns whear idoll-snakes delight
Againe to couer Satan from their sight :
  Yet these are all their gods to whome they vie
  The crocodile, the cock, the rat, the flie :
Fit gods, indeede, for such men to be scrued by.

---

1 The close of this stanza has suffered from the Editors.
  Southey misprints (line 6th) ' light' for ' night,' and
  (line 7th) ' heavy' for ' leauie '=leafy, and Cattermole
  drops (line 8th) ' vain man.' G.

22.

'The fire, the winde, the sea, the sunne, and moone,
The flitting[1] aire, and the swift-winged how'rs,
And all the watchmen, that so nimbly runne,
And centinel about the walled towers
Of the world's citie, in their heau'nly bowr's ;
    And, least their pleasant gods should want
      delight,
Neptune spues out the lady Aphrodite,
And but in Heauen proude Juno's peacocks skorne
    to lite.

23.

'The senselesse Earth, the serpent, dog, and catte,
And woorse then all these, Man, and woorst of men,
Vsurping Ioue, and swilling[2] Bacchus fat,
And drunke with the vine's purple blood; and then
The fiend himselfe they coniure from his denne,
    Because he onely yet remain'd to be
    Woorse then the worst of men: they flie from thee,
    And weare his altar-stones out with their pliant
      knee.

24.

'All that he speakes (and all he speakes are lies)
Are oracles; 'tis he (that wounded all)

---

1 Fleeting. G.
2 Richardson and Cattermole misread swelling.' G.

Cures all their wounds, he (that put out their eyes)
That giues them light, he (that death first did call
Into the world) that with his orizall¹

  Inspirits Earth : he Heau'ns al-seeing eye,
  He Earth's great prophet, he, whom rest doth
    flie,
That on salt billowes doth, as pillowes, sleeping lie

25.

' But let him in his cabin restles rest,
The dungeon of darke flames, and freezing fire,
Instice in Heau'n against man makes request
To God, and of his angels doth require
Sinne's punishment : if what I did desire,
  Or who, or against whome, or why, or whear,
  Of, or before whom ignorant I wear,
Then should my speech their sands of sins to
    mountaines rear.

26

' Were not the heau'ns pure, in whose courts I
    sue ;
The Iudge, to whom I sue, iust to requite him ;
The cause for sinne, the punishment most due ;
Iustice her selfe the plaintiffe to endite him ;

---

1 Query ' rising' as of the sun ?   But I have not met with
  the word elsewhere.   G.

The angells holy, before whom I cite him ;
  He against whom, vniust, impure ;
  Then might he sinnefull liue, and die secure,
Or triall might escape, or triall might endure.

27

' The iudge might partiall be, and ouer-pray'd ;
The place appeal'd from, in whose courts he sues ;
The fault excus'd, or punishment delay'd,
The parties selfe accus'd that did accuse ;
Angels for pardon might their praiers vse :
  But now no starre can shine, no hope be got.
  Most wretched creature, if he knewe his lot,
And yet more wretched farre, because he knowes
    it not.

28

' What should I tell how barren Earth is growne,
All for to sterue her children : didst not thou
Water with heau'nly showers her wombe vnsowne,
And drop downe cloudes[1] of flow'rs ? didst not
    thou bow
Thine easie care vnto the plowman's vowe ?
  Long might he looke, and looke, and long in
    vaine

---

1 Southey misprints ' clods.'   G.

Might load his haruest in an emptic wayne,
And beat the woods, to finde the poor okes hungrie
 graine.

29.

' The swelling Sea seethes in his angrie waucs,
And smites the Earth, that dares the traytors nou-
 rish;
Yet oft his thunder ther light corke outbraues,
Mowing the mountaines, on whose temples flourish
Whole woods of garlands; and their pride to
 cherish,
 Plowe through the seae's greene fields, and
 nets display
To catch the flying winds, and steale away,
Coozning the greedie Sea, prisning their nimble
 prey.

30.

' How often haue I scene the wauing pine,
Tost on a watrie mountaine, knocke his head
At Heau'ns too patient gates, and with salt brine
Queench the moone's burning hornes, and safely
 fled
From Heau'ns reuenge, her passengers all dead
 With stiffe astonishment tumble to Hell?
 How oft the Sea all Earth would ouerswell,
Did not thy sandie girdle binde the mightie well?

31.

'Would not the aire be fill'd with steames[1] of
   death,
To poyson the quicke[2] riuers of their blood,
Did not thy windes, fan with their panting breath,
The flitting region? would not the hastie flood
Emptie it selfe into the Sea's wide wood,   :
  Did'st not thou leade it wand'ring from his way,
  To giue men drinke, and make his waters strey,
To fresh the flowrie meadowes, through whose
   fields they play?

32.

'Who makes the sources of the siluer fountaines
From the flinth's mouth, and rocky valleis slide,
Thickning the ayrie bowells of the mountaines?
Who hath the wilde heards of the forest tide
In their cold denns, making them hungrie bide
  Till man to rest be laid? can beastly he,
  That should haue most sense, onely senseles be,
And all things else, beside himselfe, so awefull
   see?

---

1 Richardson, Southey, and Cattermole misprint 'streams.'
  . G.
2 'Living,' 'alive,' as before.   G.

I

33.

' Wear he not wilder then the saluage beast,
Prowder then haughty hills, harder then rocks,
Colder then fountaines, from their springs releas't,
Lighter then aire, blinder then senseles stocks,
More changing then the riuers curling locks :
  If reason would not, sense would soone reproouc
    him,
  And vnto shame, if not to sorrow, mooue him,
To see cold floods, wild beasts, dul stocks, hard
    stones out-loue him.

34.

' Vnder the weight of sinne the earth did fall,
And swallowed Dathan;[1] and the raging winde,
And stormie sea, and gaping whale, did call
For Iónas ;[2] and the aire did bullets finde,
And shot from Heau'n a stony showre, to grinde
  The fiue proud kings, that for their idols fought;[3]
  The sunne it selfe stood still to fight it out,[4]
And fire from heau'n flew downe, when sin to
    heau'n did shout.[5]

---

1 Numbers c. xvi.
2 Jonah i. 1 seqq. ii. 1—10, &c. G.
3 Joshua x., 11. G.
4 Joshua x., 12 seqq. G.
5 Genesis xviii., 20, and xix., 24.

35.

Should any to himselfe for safety flie?
Thè way to saue himselfe, if any were.
Wear to flie from himselfe : should he relie
Vpon the promise of his wife? but there,
What can he see, but that he most may feare,
   A syren, sweete to death : vpon his friends?
   Who that he needs, or that he hath not, lends;
Or wanting aide himselfe, ayde to another sends?

36.

His strength? but dust: his pleasure? cause of paine:
His hope? false courtier : youth or beawtie? brittle:
Intreatie? fond[1] : repentance? late, and vaine:
Iust recompence? the world wear all too little:
Thy loue? he hath no title to a tittle:
   Hell's force? in vaine her furies Hell shall
      gather:
   His seruants, kinsmen, or his children rather?
His child, if good, shall iudge; if bad, shall curse
    his father.

37.

' His life? that brings him to his end, and leaues
    him :
· His ende; that leaues him to beginne his woe:

---

1 Foolish. G.

His goods? what good in that, that so deceaues him?
His gods of wood? their feete, alas! are slowe
To goe to helpe, that must be help't to goe:
    Honour, great woorth? ah, little woorth they be
    Vnto their owners: wit? that makes him see
He wanted wit, that thought he had it, wanting
    Thee.

38.

'The Sea to drinke him quicke?'[1] that casts his
    dead:
Angells to spare? they punish: night to hide?
The world shall burne in light; the heau'ns to
    spread
Their wings to saue him? heaun it selfe shall slide,
And rowle away like melting starres, that glide
    Along their oylie threads: his minde pursues
    him:
    His house to shrowde, or hills to fall and bruse
    him?
As sergeants both attache, and witnesses accuse him.

39.

'What need I vrge, what they must needs con-
    fesse,
Sentence on them, condemn'd by their owne lust?

---

1 'Living,'. 'alive.' G.

I craue no more, and Thou canst giue no lesse,
Then death to dead men, iustice to vniust;
Shame to most shamefull, and most shameles dust:
 But if Thy mercie needs will spare her friends,
 Let Mercie there begin where Iustice endes.
'Tis cruel Mercie, that the wrong from right
 defends.'

40.

She ended, and the heau'nly Hierarchies,
Burning in zeale, thickly imbranded[1] weare;
Like to an armie that allarum cries,
And euery one shakes his ydraded[2] speare,
And the Almightie's Selfe, as He would teare
 The Earth and her firme basis quite in sunder,
 Flam'd all in iust reuenge and mightie thunder;
Heau'n stole it selfe from Earth by clouds that
 moisterd[3] vnder.

---

1 CATTERMOLE explains this as 'mustered in arms;' but
this is a mere adaptation to the context. RICHARDSON
in his great Dictionary says 'Perhaps armed with
brands,' and then quotes from Fletcher, as above.
'Brand, which means a 'torch' is also used for a
'sword,' because in motion it glitters like a burning
torch or fire-brand. Skinner. G.

2 Ydreaded *i.e.* dreaded: Richardson and Cattermole substitute 'terrific.' G.

3 Moistured, refreshed: Southey and Cattermole misprint
'moisten'd.' G.

41.

As when the cheerfull sunne, elamping[1] wide,
Glads all the world with his vprising raye,
And wooes the widow'd Earth afresh to pride,
And paint[s][2] her bosome with the flowrie Maye,
His silent sister steales him quite away,
 Wrap't in a sable clowde from mortall eyes ;
 The hastie starres at noone begin to rise,
And headlong to his early roost the sparrowe flies.

42.

But soone as he againe dishadowed is,
Restoring the blind world in his blemish't sight,
As though another day wear newely ris,[3]
The cooz'ned birds busily take their flight,
And wonder at the shortnesse of the night;
 So Mercie once againe her selfe displayes,
 Out from her sister's cloud, and open layes
Those sunshine lookes, whose beames would dim
  a thousand dayes.

---

1 Enlightening like a lamp: Cf Spenser, Fairie Queen
 III c 3 s 1: and first Sonnet. Dr. Richardson as
 before, quotes above G.

2 Misprinted 'paint': but in 1632 ed. corrected to 'paints'
 as *supra* G.

3 Richardson, Southey and Cattermole, again sadly mar
 this line, by mis-reading from the previous one 'world'
 for 'day' and 'his' for 'ris' G.

43.

How may a worme, that crawles along the dust,
Clamber the azure mountaines, thrown so high,
And fetch from thence thy faire Idea iust,
That in those sunny courts doth hidden lie,
Cloath'd with such light, as blinds the angels' eye;
   How may weake mortall euer hope to file
   His vnsmooth tongue, and his deprostrate stile?
O raise Thou from his corse Thy now entomb'd
    exile!

44.

One touch would rouze me from my sluggish
    hearse,
One word would call me to my wishèd home,
One looke would polish my afflicted verse,
One thought would steale my soule from her thicke
   • lome,
And force it wandring vp to Heau'n to come,
   Thear to importune, and to beg apace
   One happy fauour of Thy sacred grace,
To see—what though it loose her eyes?—to see
    Thy face.

45.

If any aske why roses please the sight?
Because their leaues vpon thy cheekes doe bowre:
If any aske why lillies are so white?

Because their blossoms in thy hand doe flowre :
Or why sweet plants so gratefull odours shoure?
  It is because Thy[1] breath so like they be :
Or why the Orient sunne so bright we see ?
What reason can we giue, but from Thine eies,
    and Thee ?

46.

Ros'd all in liuely crimsin ar Thy cheeks,
Whear beawties indeflourishing abide,
And, as to passe his fellowe either seekes,
Seemes both doe[2] blush at one another's pride ;
And on Thine eyelids, waiting Thee beside,
  Ten thousand Graces sit, and when they mooue
  To Earth their amourous belgards[3] from aboue,
They flie from Heau'n, and on their wings conuey
    Thy loue.

47.

All of discolour'd plumes their wings ar made,
And with so wondrous art the quills ar wrought,
That whensoere they cut the ayrie glade,
The winde into their hollowe pipes is caught :

---

1 Southey misprints 'their' G.
2 Here also misprints 'to.' G.
3 *Belles regardes* 'beautiful looks' : Richardson, as before,
  quotes Fletcher as above : Cf Spenser F Q III c 9.

As seemes the spheres with them they down haue
     brought :
  Like to the seauenfold reede of Arcadie,
  Which Pan of Syrinx made, when she did flie
To Ladon sands, and at his sighs sung merily. [1]

48.

As melting hony, dropping from the combe,
So still the words, that spring betwcen thy lipps :
Thy lippes, whear smiling Swetnesse keepes her
     home,
And heau'nly Eloquence pure manna sipps :
He that his pen but in that fountaine dipps,
  How nimbly will the golden phrases flie,
  And shed forth streames of choycest rhetorie,
Welling celestiall torrents out of poësie !

49.

Like as the thirstie land in Summer's heat,
Calls to the cloudes, and gapes at euerie showre,
As though her hungry clifts all heau'n would eat,
Which if high God into her bosome powre,
Though much refresht, yet more she could deuoure;
  So hang the greedie cars of angels sweete,
  And euery breath a thousand Cupids meete,
Some flying in, some out, and all about her fleet.

---

[1] Cf. Ovid. Met. i. 691 &c. : Virgil, Eclog. ii. 31.   G.

50.

Vpon her breast Delight doth softly sleepe,
And of Eternal Ioy is brought abed :
Those snowie mountelets, through which doe
    creepe
The milkie riuers, that ar inly bred
In siluer cisternes, and themselues do shed
  To wearie trauailers, in heat of day
  To quench their fierie thrist, and to allay
With dropping nectar floods, the furie of their way

51.

If any wander, Thou doest call him backe ;
If any be not forward, Thou incit'st him ;
Thou doest expect, if any should growe slacke ;
If any seeme but willing, thou inuit'st him ;
Or if he doe offend Thee, Thou acquit'st him ;
  Thou find'st the lost, and follow'st him that flies,
  Healing the sicke, and quickning him that dies :
Thou art the lame man's friendly staffe, the blind
    man's eyes.

52.

So faire Thou art, that all would Thee behold ;
But none can Thee behold, Thou art so faire ;
Pardon, O pardon then Thy vassal bold,
That with poore shadowes striues Thee to compare,
And match the things, which he knowes match-
    lesse are :

O Thou vive[1] mirrhour of celestiall grace,
How can fraile colours pourtraict out Thy face,
Or paint in flesh Thy beawtie in such semblance
    base ?

53.

Her vpper garment was a silken lawne,
With needle-worke richly embroidered,
Which she her selfe with her owne hand had
    drawne,
And all the world therein had pourtrayèd,
With threads so fresh and liuely colourèd,
    That seem'd the world She newe created thear,
    And the mistaken eye would rashly swear
The silken trees did growe, and the beasts liuing
    wear.

54.

Low at her feet the Earth was cast alone,
(As though to kisse Her foot it did aspire,

---

1 Richardson and Cattermole translate ' vive ' into ' living'
    and drop the ' O: '
Drummond of Hawthornden has the word and rhyme, *e.g.*
      ' O well-spring of this all,
        Thy father's image vive,
      Word, that from nought did call
        What is, doth reason, liue.'   G.

And gaue it selfe for her to tread vpon,)
With so vnlike and different attire,
That euery one that sawe it, did admire[1]
   What it might be, was of so various hewe;
   For to it selfe it oft so diuerse grewe,
That still it seem'd the same, and still it seem'd a
     newe.

55.

And here and there, few men she scattered,
(That in their thought the world esteeme but
     small
And themselues great,) but she with one fine
     thread
So short, and small, and slender, woue them all,
That like a sort of busie ants, that crawle
   About some molehill, so they wanderèd;
   And round about the wauing Sea[2] was shed:
But, for the siluer sands, small pearls were sprinklèd

56.

So curiously the vnderworke did creepe,
And curling circlets so well shadowed lay,
That afar off the waters seem'd to sleepe;
But those that neare the margin pearle did play,

Hoarcely enwaued wear with hastie sway,
  As though they meant to rocke the gentle earo
And hush the former that enslumbred wear :
And here a dangerous rocke the flying ships did
    fear.

57.

High in the ayric element there hung
Another clowdy Sea, that did disdaine
(As though his purer waues from heauen sprung)
To crawle on Earth, as doth the sluggish maine :
But it the Earth would water with his raine,
  That eb'd and flow'd, as winde and season
    would,
  And oft the Sun would cleaue the limber[1] mould
To alabaster rockes, that in the liquld rowl'd.

58.

Beneath those sunny banks, a darker cloud,
Dropping with thicker deaw, did melt apace,
And bent it selfe into a hollowe shroude,
On which, if Mercy did but cast her face,
A thousand colours did the bowe enchace,
  That wonder was to see the silke distain'd

---

1 Yielding. Cf. Milton P. L. 'wav'd their limber
fans'. VII. 476. G.

With the resplendance from her beawtie gain'd,
And Iris paint her locks with beames, so liuely
    feign'd.

59.

About her head a cyprus[1] heau'n she wore,
Spread like a veile, vpheld with siluer wire,
In which the starres so burn't in golden ore,
As seem'd the azure web was all on fire:
But hastily, to quench the sparkling ire,
  A flood of milke came rowling vp the shore,
  That on his curded waue swift Argus bore,[2]
And the immortall swan, that did her life deplore.

60

Yet strange it was, so many starres to see
Without a sunne, to give their tapers light :
Yet strange it was not, that it so should be ;
For, where the sunne centers himselfe by right,
Her face, and locks did flame, that at the sight

---

1 'Cyprus' is our modern word 'crape:' French 'c respe-
    crape.' Therefore the text is = a canopy of crape. Cf.
    Milton, Il Penseroso,
        'Sable stole of Cipres lawn
        Over thy decent shoulders draw'n.' G.
2 Southey repeats the misprint of 'wore' here, from 1632
    edn. G.

The heauenly veile, that else should nimbly
    mooue,
Forgot his flight, and all incens'd with loue
With wonder, and amazement, did her beautie
    prooue.   .

61.

Ouer her hung a canopie of state,
Not of rich tissew, nor of spangled gold,
But of a substance, though not animate,
Yet of a heaun'nly and spirituall mould,
That onely eyes of spirits might behold;
    Such light as from maine[1] rocks of diamound,
    Shooting their sparks at Phebus, would rebound,
And little angels, holding hands, daunc't all around.

62.

Seemed these little sprights, through nimbless bold,
The stately canopy bore on their wings
But them it selfe, as pendants, did vphold;
Besides the crownes of many famous kings:
Among the rest, thear Dauid euer sings,
    And now, with yeares growne young, renewes
        his layes
Vnto his golden harpe, and ditties playes,
Psalming aloud in well-tun'd songs his Maker's
    prayse.

---

1 Sea-rocks   G.

63.

Thou Self-Idea of all ioyes to come,
Whose loue is such, would make the rudest speake,
Whose loue is such, would make the wisest dumbe,
O, when wilt thou thy too-long silence breake
And ouercome the strong to saue the weake!

 If thou no weapons hast, thine eyes will wound
 Th' Almightie's selfe, that now sticke on the
  ground,
As though some blessed obiect there did them em-
  pound.

64.

Ah! miserable abiect[1] of disgrace,
What happines is in thy miserie?
I both must pittie and enuie thy case;
For she that is the glorie of the skie,
Leaues heauen blind, to fix on thee her eye.

 Yet her (though Mercie's selfe esteems not
  small)
 The world despis'd; they her Repentance call,
And she herselfe despises, and the world, and all.

65.

Deepely, alas! empassionèd she stood,
To see a flaming brand, tost vp from hell,

---

1 Southey misprints 'object.'   G.

Boyling her heart in her owne lustfull blood,
That oft for torment she would loudely yell;
Nowe sho would sighing sit, and nowe she fell
   Crouching vpon the ground, in sackcloath trust:[1]
   Early and late she prayed, and fast she must.
And all her haire hung full of ashes, and of dust.

66.

Of all most hated, yet hated most of all
Of her owne selfe she was; disconsolat
(As though her flesh did but infunerall
Her buried ghost) sho in an arbour[2] sat
Of thornie brier, weeping her cursed state;
   And her before, a hastie river fled,
   Which her blind eyes with faithfull penance
      fed,
And all about, the grasse with tears hung downe
   his head.

67.

Her eyes, though blind abroad, at home kept
   fast;
Inwards they turn'd, and look't into her head:
At which shee often started, as aghast
To see so fearfull spectacles of dread;

---

1 Trussed *ie* dressed or girded. G.

2 Southey has 'harbour' G.

J

And with one hand, her breast she martyred,
  Wounding her heart, the same to mortifie;
  The other a faire damsel held her by,
Which if but once let go, shee sunke immediatly.

68.

But Faith was quicke and nimble as the heau'n,
As if of loue and life shee all had been,
And though of present sight her sense were reauen,
Yet shee could see the things could not be seen:
Beyond the starres, as nothing wear between,
  She fixt her sight, disdeigning things belowe:
  Into the Sea she could a mountaine throwe,
And make the sun to stande, and waters backewards
    flowe.

69.

Such when as Mercie her beheld from high,
In a darke valley, drown'd with her owne tears,
One of her Graces she sent hastily,
Smiling Eirene,[1] that a garland wears
Of guilded oliue, on her fairer hears,[2]
  To crowne the fainting soules true sacrifice;
  Whom when as sad Repentance comming spies,
The holy Desperado wip't her swollen eyes.

---

1 Peace. G.   2 Hairs. G.

70.

But Mercie felt a kinde remorse to runne
Through her soft vaines, and therefore, hying fast
To giue an end to silence, thus begunne :—
'Aye-honour'd Father, if no ioy Thou hast
But to reward desert, reward at last
   The deuil's voice, spoke with a serpent's tongue,—
   Fit to hisse out the words so deadly stung,—
And let him die, death's bitter charmes so sweetely
     sung.

71.

'He was the father of that hopeles season,
That, to serue other gods, forgot their owne :
The reason was, Thou wast aboue their reason :
They would haue any[1] gods, rather then none,
A beastly serpent, or a senselesse stone :
   And these, as Iustice hates, so I deplore ;
   But the vp-plowed heart, all rent and tore,
Though wounded by it selfe, I gladly would re-
     store.

72.

'He was but dust; why fear'd he not to fall ?
And, beeing fall'n, how can he hope to liue ?

---

1 Southey misprints 'other.' G.

Cannot the hand destroy him, that made all?
Could He not take away, as well as giue?
Should man deprave, and should not God depriue?
　Was it not all the world's deceiuing spirit,
　(That, bladder'd vp with pride of his owne merit,
Fell in his rise) that him of Heau'n did disinherit?

73.

' He was but dust: how could he stand before
　　Him?
And being fall'n, why should he feare to die?
Cannot the hand that made him first, restore him?
Deprau'd of sinne, should he depriued lie
Of grace? can He not hide[1] infirmitie
　That gaue him strength? vnworthy the forsaking,
　He is, who euer weighs, without mistaking,
Or Maker of the man, or manner of his making.

74.

' Who shall Thy temple incense any more?
Or at Thy altar crowne the sacrifice?
Or strewe with idle flow'rs the hallow'd flore?
Or what should prayer deck with hearbs and spice
Her vialls, breathing orisons of price?
　If all must paie that which all cannot paie?

---

1 Southey misprints 'find.'   G.

O first begin with mee, and Mercie slaie,
And Thy thrice honour'd Sonne, that now beneath
    doth strey.

75.

'But if or He or I, may liue, and speake,
And Heau'n can ioye to see a sinner weepe;
Oh let not Iustice yron sceptre breake
A heart alreadie broke; that lowe doth creep,
And with prone humblesse her feets' dust doth
    sweep.
  Must all goe by desert? is nothing free?
  Ah! if but those that onely woorthy be,
None should Thee euer see, none should Thee euer
  see.

76.

'What hath man done, that man shall not vndoe,
Since God to him is growne so neer a kin?
Did his foe slay him? He shall slay his foe:
Hath he lost all? He all againe shall win:
Is sinne his master? He shall master sinne:
  Too hardy soule, with sinne the field to trie:
  The onely way to conquer, was to flie;
But thus long Death hath liu'd, and now Death's
  selfe shall die.

77

' He is a path, if any be misled,
He is a robe, if any naked bee;
If any chaunce to hunger, He is bread,
If any be a bondman, He is free,
If any be but weake, howe strong is Hee!
  To dead men life He is, to sicke men health,
  To blinde men sight, and to the needie wealth;
A pleasure without losse, a treasure without stealth.

78

' Who can forget—neuer to be forgot—
The time, that all the world in slumber lies,
When, like the starres, the singing angels shot
To Earth, and Heau'n awakèd all his eyes,
To see another sunne at midnight rise
  On Earth? Was neuer sight of pareil[1] fame;
  For God before, man like himselfe, did frame,
But God himselfe now like a mortall man became.

79

A Child He was, and had not learn't to speake,
That with His word the world before did make;
' His mother's armes Him bore, He was so weake,

---

1 'Equal.' G.

That with one hand the vaults of Heau'n could
    shake;
See how small roome my infant Lord doth take,
  Whom all the world is not enough to hold!
  Who of His yeares, or of His age hath told?
Neuer such age so young, neuer a child so old.

80

'And yet but newely He was infanted,
And yet alreadie He was sought to die;
Yet scarcely borne, alreadie banishèd
Not able yet to goe, and forc't to flie:
But scarcely fled away, when, by and by,
  The tyrant's[1] sword with blood is all defil'd,
  And Rachel, for her sonnes, with furie wild,
Cries, 'O thou cruell king, and, O my sweetest
    child!'

81

'Egypt his nource became, whear Nilus springs,
Who streit to entertaine, the rising sunne
The hasty haruest in his bosome brings;
But now for drieth[2] the fields wear all vndone,
And now with waters all is ouerrunne:

---

1 Misprinted 'tyrans' but corrected in 1632 edn. G.
2 Drought. G.

So fast the Cynthian mountaines powr'd their
     snowe,

When once they felt the sunne so neere them
     glowe,

That Nilus Egypt lost, and to a sea did growe.

82

' The angells caroll'd lowd their song of peace ;

The cursed oracles wear strucken dumb ;[1]

To see their Sheapheard, the poore sheapheards
     press ;

To soe their King, the kingly sophies[2] come ;

And them to guide vnto his Master's home,

    A starre comes dauncing vp the Orient,

    That springs for ioye over the strawy tent,

Whear gold, to make their prince a crowne, they
     all present.

83.

" Young John, glad child ! before he could be borne,

Leapt in the woombe, his ioy to prophecie :[3]

---

1 Cf: Milton's Ode ' on the Morning of Christ's Nativity'
    stanza 19

      ' The Oracles are dum,

      No voice or hideous humm

        Runs through the arched roof'....... .. G.

2 Wise men. Cf Milton, P. L. X. 435 ' Bactrian Sophi' G.

3 St. Luke i. 41. G.

Old Anna, though with age all spent and worne,
Proclaimes her Sauiour to posteritie :[1]
And Simeon fast his dying notes doeth plie.[2]
   Oh, how the blessed soules about Him trace !
   It is the Sire[3] of heau'n thou doest embrace :
Sing, Simeon, sing—sing, Simeon, sing apace ! '

84.

With that the mightie thunder dropt away
From God's vnwarie[4] arme, now milder growne,
And melted into teares : as if to pray
For pardon, and for pittie, it had knowne,
That should haue been for sacred vengeance
     throwne :
   Thereto the armies angelique devo'wd
   Their former rage, and all to Mercie bow'd ;
Their broken weapons at her feet they gladly
     strow'd.

---

1 St. Luke II. 36 G.
2 St. Luke II. 29. G.
3 Southey misprints 'fire' G.
4 Query=unweary, not worn out ? 'Unwary '=unwatch-
   ful, unexpecting, seems over-bold. But see The Purple
   Island' canto VI. stanza 19, line 4 where this special
   bit is finely praised. G.

85.

' Bring, bring, ye Graces, all your silver flaskets,
Painted with euery choicest flowre that growes,
That I may soone vnflow'r your fragrant baskets,
To strowe the fields with odours whear he goes,
Let what so e're He treads on be a rose.'
   So downe shee let her eyelids fall, to shine
   Vpon the rivers of bright Palestine,
Whose woods drop honie, and her rivers skip with
    wine.

CHRIST'S
VICTORIE AND TRIUMPH.

THE ARGUMENT.

Christ brought into the place of combat, the wildernes, among the wilde beasts: Mark I., 13 : st. 1.—Described by His proper attribute, the Mercie of God : st. 2, 3—Whom the creatures cannot but adore : st. 4, 5,—by His unitie with the Godhead : st. 6.—His proper place : st. 7.—The beautie of His body, Cant. V., 11 ; Psal, XLV., 2 ; Gen. XLIX., 13 ; Cant. V., 10 ; and Isa. LIII., 2 : st. 8—15.—By preparing Himself to the combate with His adversarie that seem'd what he was not : st. 14, 15.—Some devout Essene : st. 16—19.—closely tempting him to despaire of God's prouidence, and prouide for Himself : st. 23,—But was what He seemed not, Satan, and would faine haue lead Him, 1—To Desperation, characterd by His place, countenance, apparell, horrible apparitions, &c.: st. 21—30.—2—To Presumption : character'd by her place, attendants , &c.: st. 31—36.— and by her temptation st. 37.—3—To Vainglorie : poetically described from the place where her court stood ; a garden : st. 38—49,—from her court and courtiers : st. 51.—(1.) Pleasure in Drinking : st. 50, 51 ; in Luxury: st. 52; (2.) Avarice : st. 53—55 ; (3.) Ambitious honour : st. 56; from her throne, [and] from her temptation : st. 57—69.—The effect of this victorie in Satan : st. 60 ; the angels : st. 61 ; the creatures : st. 62.

CHRIST'S VICTORIE ON EARTH.

1.

THEAR, all alone, she spi'd, alas the while!
In shadie darknes, a poore Desolate,
That now had measur'd many a wearie mile,
Through a wast desert, whither heau'nly fate
And His owne will, Him brought; He praying
    sate.
    And Him to prey, as He to pray began,[1]
    The citizens of the wilde forrest ran,
And all with open throat would swallowe whole
    the man.

2.

Soone did the Ladie to her Graces crie,
And on their wings her selfe did nimbly strowe,
After her coach a thousand Loues did flie;
So downe into the wildernesse they throwe;

---

1 Cf. Fuller:
    'On her that pray'd so long, doth prey at last,'
        'DAVID'S HEAVIE PUNISHMENT: st. 14.' G.

Whear she, and all her trayne that with her flowe
  Thorough the ayrie waue, with sailes so gay.
  Sinking into His brest that wearie lay,
Made shipwracke of themselues, and vanish't quite
    away.

3.

.Seemed that Man had them devoured all,
  Whome to deuoure the beasts had made pretence;
But Him their saluage thirst did nought appall,
  Though weapons none He had for His defence:
  What armes for Innocence, but innocence?
    For when they saw their Lord's bright cogni-
      zance
    Shine in His face, soone did they disadvaunce
And some vnto Him kneele, and some about Him
    daunce.

4.

Downe fell the lordly lion's angrie mood,
And he himselfe fell downe in congies[1] lowe;
Bidding Him welcome to his wastfull wood;
Sometime he kist the grasse whear He did goe,
And, as to wash His feete he well did knowe,
  With fauning tongue he lickt away the dust;
  And euery one would neerest to Him thrust,
And euery one, with new, forgot his former lust.

---

1 Bows = salutations. G.

5.

Vnmindfull of himselfe, to minde his Lord,
The lamb stood gazing by the tyger's side,
As though betweene them they had made accord;
And on the lion's back the goate did ride,
Forgetfull of the roughnes of the hide :
    If He stood still, their eyes vpon Him bayted,
    If walkt, they all in order on Him wayted,
And when He slept, they as His watch themselues
      conceited.

6.

Wonder doeth call me vp to see—(O no,
I cannot see,—and therefore sinke in woonder)
The Man that shines as bright as God,—not so,
For God He is Himselfe, that close lies vnder
That Man,—. so close, that no time can dissunder
    That band ; yet not so close, but from Him
      breake
    Such beames, as mortall eyes are all too weake
Such sight to see,—or it, if they should see, to
      speake.

7

Vpon a grassie hillock He was laid,
With woodie primroses befreckeled;
Ouer His head the wanton shadowes plaid
Of a wilde oliue, that her bowghs so spread,

As with her leau's she seem'd to crowne His head,
 And her greene armes to embrace the Prince of
  Peace ;
 The sunne so neere, needs must the Winter
  cease,
The sunne so neere, another Spring seem'd to in-
  crease.

8

His haire was blacke, and in small curls did twine,
As though it wear the shadowe of some light;
And vnderneath, His face, as day did shine—
But sure the day shinèd not halfe so bright,
Nor the sunne's shadowe made so darke a night.
 Vnder His louely locks, her head to shroude,
 Did make[1] Humilitie her selfe growe proude :—
Hither, to light their lamps, did all the Graces
  croude.

9.

One of ten thousand soules I am, and more,
That of His eyes, and their sweete wounds com-
  plaine :
Sweete are the wounds of Loue, neuer so sore—
Ah ! might He often slaie me so againe !

---

1 Cattermole reads 'meek' G.

Ho neuer liues that thus is neuer slaine.
What boots it watch? those eyes for all my art,
Mine owne eyes looking on, haue stole my heart:
In them Loue bends his bowe, and dips his burning
    dart.

10.

As when the sunne, caught in an aduerse clowde,
Flies crosse the world, and thear a new begets
The watry picture of his beautie proude :
Throwes all abroad his sparckling spangelets,[1]
And the whole world in dire amazement sets,
    To see two dayes abroad at once ; and all
    Doubt whether nowe he rise, or now will[2] fall :
So flam'd the Godly flesh, proude of his heau'nly
    thrall.

11.

His cheekes as snowie apples, sop't in wine,
Had their red roses quencht with lillies white,
And like to garden strawberries did shine,
Wash't in a bowle of milk, or rose-buds bright
Vnbosoming their brests against the light :

---

1 Spangles = rays of sunlight broken into drops, *ie* dimi-
    nutive of ' spangles.' G.
2 Richardson and Cattermole misprint ' he.' G.

Here loue-sick soules did eat, thear dranke, and
    made
Sweete-smelling posies, that could neuer fade,—
But worldly eyes Him thought more like some
    liuing shade.

12.

For Laughter neuer look't upon His browe,
Though in His face all smilling ioyes did bide :
No silken banners did about Him flowe—
Fooles make their fetters ensignes of their pride :
He was the best cloath'd when naked was His side. [1]
    A Lambe He was, and wollen fleece He bore, [2]
    Wouo with one thread : His feete low sandalls
        wore ;
But bared were his legges,—so went the times of
    yore.

13

As two white marble pillars that vphold
God's holy place, whear He in glorie sets,
And rise with goodly grace and courage bold,

---

1 Cf. Fuller
    'Who most was nak't when cloathèd in his weeds'
    'David's Heavie Punishment' III. 6. See also the
    first of his before unpublished Epigrams. G.
2 Richardson and Cattermole misprint 'wore' G.

To beare his temple on their ample ietts,[1]
   Vein'd euery whear with azure rivulets:
   Whom all the people on some holy morne,
   With boughs and flowrie garlands doe[2] adorne—
Of such, though fairer farre, this temple was vp-
     borne.

14

Twice had Diana bent her golden bowe,
And shot from hea'un her siluer shafts, to rouse
The sluggish saluages, that den belowe,
And all the day in lazie couuert drouze,
Since Him the silent wildernesse did house:
   The heau'n His roofe and arbour harbour was,
   The ground His bed, and His moist pillowe, grasse;
But fruit thear none did growe, nor riuers none did
     passe.

15

At length an aged syre farre off He sawe
Come slowely footing; euerie step he guest
One of his feete he from the graue did drawe;
Three legges he had—the wooden was the best;[3]

---

1 'Projections': it occurs thus in Sir John Davies. G.
2 Southey misprints 'to' G.
3 'You are now come to go on three legs:' Livesey's
  Greatest Loss,' as before. G.

And all the waie he went, he euer blest
  With benedicities, and prayers store ;
  But the bad ground was blesèd ne'r the more;
And all his head with snowe of age was waxen hore.

16

A good old hermit he might seeme to be,
That for deuotion had the world forsaken,
And now was trauailing some saint to see,
Since to his beads he had himselfe betaken,
Whear all his former sinnes he might awaken,
  And them might wash away with dropping brine,
  And almes, and fasts, and churche's discipline ;
And dead, might rest his bones vnder the holy
    shrine.

17.

But when he neerer came, he lowted lowe
With prone obeysance, and with curt'sie kinde,
That at his feete his head he seemd to throwe ;—
What needs him now another saint to finde ?
Affections are the sailes, and faith the wind,
  That to this saint a thousand soules conueigh
  Each hour : O happy pilgrims thither strey !
What caren they for beasts, or for the wearie way?

18.

Soone the old palmer his deuotions sung,
Like pleasing anthems, moduled in time ;

For well that aged syre could tip his tongue
With golden foyle of eloquence, and lime,
And licke his rugged speech with phrases prime.
 ' Ay me, quoth he, how many yeares haue beene,
  Since these old eyes the sunne of heau'n haue
   seene!
Certes the Sonne of Heau'n they now behold, I
  weene.

19

' Ah, mote my humble cell so blessed be,
As Heau'n to welcome in his lowely roofe,
And be the Temple for Thy Deitie!
Loe how my cottage worships Thee aloofe,
That vnder ground hath hid his head, in proofe
 It doth adore Thee with the seeling lowe—
  Here honie, milke, and chesnuts wild doe growe;
The boughs a bed of leaues vpon Thee shall
  bestowe.

20.

'But oh! he said, and therewith sigh't full deepe,—
The heau'ns, alas! too enuious are growne,
Because our fields Thy presence from them keepe;
For stones doe growe where corne was lately sown:
(So stooping downe, he gather'd vp a stone:)
 But Thou with corne canst make this stone to
  eare.

What needen[1] we the angrie heau'ns to feare?
Let them enuie vs still, so we enioy Thee here.'

21.

Thus on they wandred: but those holy weeds
A monstrous serpent, and no man, did couer:
So vnder greenest hearbs the adder feeds:
And round about that stinking corps did houer
The dismall prince of gloomie night, and ouer
   His euer-damned head the Shadowes err'd[2]
   Of thousand pecant ghosts, vnseene, vnheard,
And all the Tyrant feares—and all the Tyrant
    fear'd.

22.

He was the sonne of blackest Acheron,
Whear many frozen soules doe chattring lie,
And rul'd the burning waues of Phlegethon,
Whear many more in flaming sulphur frie,
At once compel'd to liue, and fore't to die;
   Whear nothing can be heard for the loud crie
   Of ' Oh!' and ' Ah!' and ' Out alas! that I
Or once againe might liue, or once at length might
    die!'

---

1 Richardson and Cattermole misread 'What need we
their....' G.
2 Wandered = hovered. G.

23.

Ere long they came neere to a balefull bowre,
Much like the mouth of that infernall caue,
That gaping stood, all commers to deuoure.
"Darke, dolefull, dreary,—like a dreary graue,
That still for carrion carkasses doth craue :"[1]
 The ground no hearbs but venomous, did beare,
 Nor ragged trees did leaue, but euery whear
Dead bones and skulls wear cast, and bodies hanged
 wear.

24.

Vpon the roofe the bird of sorrowe sat
Elonging[2] ioyfull day with her sad note,
And through the shady aire, the fluttring bat
Did waue her leather sayles, and blindely flote ;
While with her wings the fatall shreech-owle smote
 Th' vnblessed house ; thear, on a craggy stone,
 Celeno[3] hung, and made his direfull mone,
And all about the murdered ghosts did shreek and
 grone.

25.

Like clowdie moonshine, in some shadowie groue
Such was the light in which Despaire did dwell ;

---

1 Spenser : F. Q., B. I., c. 9., st. 33. G.

2 Lengthening : Dr. Richardson, as before, quotes Fletcher
above. G.

3 Celaeno : one of the harpies. Cf. Æneid. iii., 211. G.

But he himselfe with night for darknesse stroue.
His black uncombèd locks dishevell'd fell
About his face ; through which, as brands of Hell,
  Sunk in his skull, his staring eyes did glowe,
    That made him deadly looke; their glimpse did
      showe
Like cockatrice's eyes, that sparks of poyson throwe.

26.

His cloaths wear ragged clouts, with thornes pind
    fast ;
And, as he musing lay, to stonie fright
A thousand wild Chimeras would him cast :
As when a fearefull dreame, in mid'st of night,
Skips to the braine, and phansies to the sight
  Some wingèd furie, strait the hasty foot,
  Eger[1] to flie, cannot plucke vp his root,
    The voyce dies in the tongue, and mouth gapes
      without boot[2]

27.

Now he would dreame that he from heauen fell,
And then would snatch the ayre, afraid to fall ;
And now he thought he sinking was to hell,
And then would grasp the earth ; and now his stall

---

1 Eager. G.
2 To no purpose = dumb. G.

Him seemèd Hell, and then he out would crawle;
  And euer, as he crept, would squint aside,
  Lest him, perhaps, some furie had espide,
And then, alas! he should in chaines for euer bide.

28.

Therefore he softly shrunke, and stole away,
Ne euer durst to drawe his breath for feare,
Till to the doore he came, and thear he lay
Panting for breath, as though he dying were;
And still he thought he felt their craples teare[1]
  Him by the heels backe to his ougly denne;
  Out faine he would haue leap't abroad, but then
The Heau'n, as Hell he fear'd, that punish guilty
    men.

29.

Within the gloomic hole of this pale wight
The serpent woo'd Him with his charmes to inne;
Thear He might baite the day, and rest the night:
But vnder that same baite a fearful grin[2]
Was readie to intangle Him in sinne,

---

1 'Claws:' Spenser F. Q. v. 8. 40. G.
2 = Gin or trap, as in the English Bible of 1611 in Job
    xviii, 9: Psalms, cxl., 5: cxli., 9. Consult Mr. W.
    Aldis Wright's inestimable 'Bible Word-Book' under

But He vpon ambrosia daily fed,
That grew in Eden, thus He answerèd:
So both away wear caught, and to the Temple fled.

30.

Well knewe our Sauiour this the serpent was,
And the Old Serpent knewe our Sauiour well;
Neuer did any this in falshood passe,
Neuer did any Him in truth excell:
With Him we fly to Heau'n, from Heau'n we fell
    With him: but nowe they both together met
    Vpon the sacred pinnacles, that threat,
With their aspiring tops, Astræa's starrie seat.

31

Here did Presvmption her pauillion spread,
Ouer the Temple, the bright starres among;
(Ah! that her foot should trample on the head
Of that most reuerend place!) and a lewd throng
Of wanton boyes sung her a pleasant song
    Of loue, long life, of mercie, and of grace;
    And euery one her deerely did embrace,
And she herselfe enamour'd was of her owne face.

'gin.' No one who values genuine help toward
better Bible-knowledge will go without this 'Word-
Book.' It is truly *multum in parvo*. G.

32

A painted face, belied with vermeyl store,
Which light Euëlpis[1] euery day did trimme,
That in one hand a guilded anchor wore ;
Not fixed on the rocke, but on the brimme
Of the wide aire, she let it loosely swimme :
Her other hand a sprinkle[2] carried,
And euer, when her Ladie wauerèd,
Court holy-water all vpon her sprinkeled.

33.

Poor foole ! she thought herselfe in wondrous price
With God, as if in Paradise she wear ;
But, wear she not in a foole's paradise,
She might haue seen more reason to despere :
But Him she, like some ghastly fiend, did feare ;
And therefore, as that wretch hew'd out his cell
Vnder the bowels, in the heart of Hell,
So she aboue the moon, amid the starres would dwell.

---

1 'Good Hope' personified: I have not found it elsewhere
  Cf. 'The Purple Island,' c. ix., st. 32, where she is
  personified as Elpinus. G.
2 A vessel having a 'rose' for scattering water finely, as
  used in a garden: here perhaps the thing used in
  Roman Catholic churches for 'sprinkling' holy water.

34.

Her tent wlth sunny cloudes was seel'd aloft,
And so exceeding shone with a false light,
That heau'n it selfe to her it seemèd oft;
Heau'n without cloudes to her deluded sight,
But cloudes withouten heau'n it was aright;
    And as her house was built, so did her braine
    Build castles in the aire, with idle paine,
But heart she neuer had in all her body vaine.

35.

Like as a ship in which no ballance[1] lies,
Without a pilot, on the sleeping waues,
Fairely along with winde and water flies,
And painted masts with silken sayles embraues,[2]
That Neptune ['s] selfe the bragging vessel saues,
    To laugh a while at her so proud aray;
    Her wauing streamers loosely shee lets play,
And flagging colours shine as bright as smiling day:

36.

But all so soone as heau'n his browes doth bend,
She veils her banners, and pulls in her beames,
The emptic barke the raging billows send
Vp to the Olympique waues, and Argus seemes

Againe to ride vpon our lower streames:
  Right so Presvmption did her selfe behaue,
  Tossèd about with euery stormie waue,
And in white lawne shee went, most like an angel
  braue.

37.

Gently our Sauiour shee began to shrive,[1]
Whether He wear the Sonne of God, or no;
For any other she disdeign'd to wiue:
And if He wear, shee bid Him fearles throw
Himselfe to ground; and thearwithall did show
  A flight of little angels, that did wait,
  Vpon their glitttering wings, to latch[2] Him strait,
And longèd on their backs to feele His glorious
  weight.

38.

But when she saw her speech preuailèd nought,
Her selfe she tombled headlong to the flore:
But Him tho angels on their feathers caught,
And to an ayric mountaine nimbly bore,
Whose snowie shoulders, like some chaulkie shore,

---

1 To examine as a confessor. G.
2 Catch: Dr. Richardson, as before, quotes Fletcher above
  Richardson and Cattermole misread 'launch' G.

Restles Olympus seem'd to rest vpon,
With all his swimming globes: so both are
    gone,
The Dragon with the Lamb—Ah! vnmeet paragon!

39.

All suddenly the hill his snowe deuours,
In liew whereof a goodly garden grew,
As if the snow had melted into flow'rs,
Which their sweet breath in subtill vapours threw,
That all about perfumèd spirits flew:
    For what so euer might aggrate the sense,
    In all the world, or please the appetence,
Heer it was powred out in lavish affluence.

40.

Not louely Ida might with this compare,
Though many streames his banks besiluered;
Though Xanthus with his golden sands he bare,
Nor Hibla,[1] though his thyme depasturèd
As fast againe with honie blossomèd;
    Ne Rhodope, ne Tempe's flow'ry playne:
    Adonis' garden was to this but vayne,
Though Plato on his beds a flood of praise did
    rayne.

---

1 Hybla. G.

41.

For in all these, some one thing most did grow,
But in this one, grew all things elso beside;
For sweet Varietie herselfo did throw
To euery banke: here all the ground she dide
In lillie white; there pinks eblazed wide;
  And damask't all the earth; and here shee shed
  Blew violets, and there came roses red;
And euery sight the yeelding sense, as captiue led.

42.

The garden like a ladie faire was cut,
That lay as if shee slumber'd in delight,
And to the open skies her eyes did shut;
The azure fields of heau'n wear 'sembled right
In a large round, set with the flow'rs of light:
  The flowr's-de-luce, and the round sparks of
    deaw,
  That hung vpon the azure leaues, did shew
Like twinkling starrs, that sparkle in th' eau'ning
  blew.

43.

Vpon a hillic banke her head shee cast,
On which the bowre of Vaine-delight was built;
White and red roses for her face wear plac't,
And for her tresses marigolds wear spilt:

Them broadly shee displaid, like flaming guilt,
   Till in the ocean the glad day wear drown'd;
   Then vp againe her yellow locks she wound,
And with greene filletts in their prettie calls[1] them
    bound.

44.

What should I here depeint her lillie hand,
Her veines of violets, her ermine brest,
Which thear in orient colours liuing stand;
Or how her gowne with silken leaues is drest;
Or how her watchmen, arm'd with boughie crest,
   A wall of prim[2] hid in his bushes bears,[8]
   Shaking at euery winde their leauie spears,
While she supinely sleeps, ne to be wakèd fears!

45.

Ouer the hedge depends the graping[4] elme,
Whose greener head empurpuled in wine,
Seeméd to wonder at his bloodie helme,
And halfe suspect the bunches of the vine;
Least they, perhaps, his wit should vndermine.

---

1 Caul = small caps. Cf. Aldis Wright, as before. G.
2 Privet. G.
3 Bearings = fruit? G.
3 = grape-supporting. G.

For well he knewe such fruit he neuer bore:
But her weake armes embracèd him the more,
And with her ruby grapes laught at her para-
  . mour.

46.

Vnder the shadowe of these drunken elmes
A fountaine rose, where Pangloretta vses
(When her some flood of fancie ouerwhelms,
And one of all her fauorites she chuses)
To bath herselfe, whom she in lust abuses,
    And from his wanton body sucks his soule,
     Which, drown'd in pleasure in that shaly[1] bowle
And swimming in delight, doth amarously rowle![2]

47.

The font of siluer was, and so his showrs
In siluer fell, onely the guilded bowles
(Like to a fornace, that the min'rall powres)
Seem'd to haue moul't it in their shining holes;
And on the water, like to burning coles,
    On liquid siluer, leaues of roses lay:
    But when Panglorie here did list to play,
Rose-water then it ranne, and milke it rain'd they
  say.

---

1 Shallow. G.

2 Nearly all this stanza is omitted by Cattermole. G.

48.

The roofe thicke cloudes did paint, from which
    three boyes
Three 'gaping mermaides with their 'eawrs[1] did
    feed,
Whose brests let fall the streame, with sleepie
    noise,
To lions mouths, from whence it leapt with speede,
And in the rosie lauer seem'd to bleed.
    The naked boyes vnto the water's fall,
    Their stonie nightingales had taught to call,
When Zephyr breath'd into their watry interall

49.

And all about, embayéd in soft sleepe,
A heard of charméd beasts aground were spread,
Which the faire witch in goulden chaines did keepe,
And them in willing bondage fettcrèd;
Once men they liu'd, but now the men were dead,
    And turn'd to beasts; so fabled Homer old,
    That Circe. with her potion, charm'd in gold,
Vs'd manly soules in beastly bodies to immould.

50.

Through this false Eden, to his leman's bowre,
(Whome thousand soules devoutly idolize)

---

1 Ewers = vases. G.

Our first destroyer led our Sauiour:
Thear in the lower roome, in solemne wise,
They daunc't around, aud powr'd their sacrifice
   To plumpe Lyæus,[1] and among the rest,
   The iolly priest, in yuie garlands drest,
Chaunted wild orgialls, in honour of tho feast.

51

Others within their arbours swilling sat,
(For all the roome about was arbourèd)
With laughing Bacchus, that was growne so fat,
That stand he could not, but was carrièd,
And. euery euening freshly watcrèd,
   To quench his fierie cheeks, and all about
   Small cocks broke through the wall, and
      sallied out
Flagons of wine, to set on fire that spueing rout.

52.

·This their inhumèd soules esteem'd their wealths,
To crowne the bouzing kan from day to night,
And sicke to drinke themselues, with drinking
      healths ;
Some vomitting, all drunken with delight.
Hence to a loft, carv'd all in yvorie white,

---

1 Bacchus. G.

They came, whear whiter ladies naked went,
Melted in pleasure and soft languishment,
And sunke in beds of roses, amourous glaunces
    sent.[1]

53.

Flie, flie, Thou holy Child, that wanton roome!
And thou, my chaster Muse, those harlots shun,
And with Him to a higher storie come,
Whear mounts of gold, and flouds of siluer run,
The while the owners, with their wealth vndone,
    Starve in their store, and in their plenty pine,
    Tumbling themselues vpon their heaps of mine,[2]
Glutting their famish't soules with the deceitful
    shine.

54.

Ah! who was he such pretious perills found?
How strongly Nature did her treasures hide,
And threw vpon them mountains of thicke ground,
To darke their orie lustre! but queint Pride
Hath taught her sonnes to wound their mother's
    side,

---

1 Cattermole drops out st. 51 & 52 without indicating the
   omission. G.
2 =Heaps from the mine. G.
3 Richardson and Cattermole misread 'him   G

And gage[1] the depth, to search for flaring shells,
In whose bright bosome spumie[2] Bacchus swells,
That neither heau'n nor earth henceforth in safetie
 dwells.

55,

O sacred hunger of the greedie eye,
Whose neede hath end, but no end covetise,
Emptie in fulnes, rich in pouertie,
That hauing all things, nothing can suffice,
How thou befanciest the men most wise!
 The poore man would be rich, the rich man
  great,
 The great man king, the king, in God's owne seat
Enthron'd, with mortal arme dares flames and
  thunder threat.

56.

Therefore aboue the rest Ambition sat;
His court with glitterant pearle was all enwall'd,
And round about the wall in chaires of state,
And most majestique splendor, were enstall'd

---

2 Gauge. G.
´3 Foamy: Dr. Richardson as before, quotes Fletcher
 above. Cf. Milton P.L. vi. 479 'fierie spume.' G.

A hundred kings, whose temples wear impal'd
  In goulden diadems, set here and thear
  With diamounds, and gemmed euerywhear,
And of their golden virges[1] none disceptred wear.

57.

High over all Panglorie's blazing throne,
In hen bright turret, all of christal wrought,
Like Phæbus lampe, in midst of heauen, shone;
Whose starry top with pride infernall fraught,
Selfe-arching columns to vphold wear taught:
  In which her image still reflected was
  By the smooth christall, that, most like her
    glasse,
In beauty and in frailtie, did all others passe.

58.

A siluer wande the sorceresse did sway,
And, for a crowne of gold, her haire she wore;
Onely a garland of rose-buds did play
About her locks; and in her hand she bore
A hollowe globe of glasse, that long before
  She full of emptinesse had bladdered,
  And all the world therein depicturèd:
Whose colours, like the rainbowe, euer vanishèd.

---

1 Rods : Dr. Richardson here also quotes Fletcher. G.

59.

Such watry orbicles[1] young boyes do blowe
Out of their sopy shels, and much admire
The swimming world, which tenderly they rowe
With easie breath, till it be waued higher :
But if they chaunce but roughly once aspire,
   The painted bubble instantly doth fall.
   Here when she came, she 'gan for musique call,
And sung this wooing song, to welcome Him
     withall :—

Loue is the blossome whear thear blowes
Euery thing that liues or growes :
Loue doth make the heau'ns to moue,
And the sun doth burne in loue :
Loue the strong and weake doth yoke,
And makes the yuie climbe the oke ;
Vnder whose shadowes lions wilde,
Soft'ned by loue, grow tame and mild ;
Loue no med'cine can appease,
He burnes the fishes in the seas ;
Not all the skill his wounds can stench,[2]

---

1 Soap-bubbles. Dr. Richardson, as before quotes Fletcher
  above. G.
2 Staunch. G.

Not all the sea his fire can quench:
Loue did make the bloody spear
Once a leuie coat to wear,
While in his leaues thear shrouded lay
Sweète birds, for loue, that sing and play:
And of all loue's ioyfull flame,
I the bud and blossome am:
    Onely bend Thy knee to mee,
    Thy wooing shall Thy winning bee.

See, see the flowers that belowe,
Now as fresh as morning blowe;
And of all, the virgin rose,
That as bright Aurora showes:
How they all vnleaued die,
Loosing their virginitie;
Like vnto a summer-shade,
But now borne, and now they fade.
Euery thing doth passe away,
Thear is danger in delay:
Come, come gather then the rose,
Gather it, or it you lose:
All the sand of Tagus'. shore
Into my bosome casts his ore:
All the valleys' swimming corne
To my house is yeerely borne;
Euery grape of euery vine

Is gladly bruis'd to make me wine,
While ten thousand kings, as proud,
To carry vp my train haue bow'd,
And a world of ladies send me
In my chambers to attend me:
All the starres in heau'n that shine,
And ten thousand more, are mine.
    Onely bend Thy knee to mee,
    Thy wooing shall Thy winning bee.

60.

Thus sought the dire Enchauntress in His minde
Her guilefull bayt to haue embosomèd;
But He her charmes dispersèd into winde,
And her of insolence admonishèd;
And all her optique glasses shatterèd.
    So with her sire to Hell shee took her flight,
    (The starting ayre flew from the damned spright,)
Whear deeply both[1] aggriev'd, plunged themselues
      in night.

61.

But to their Lord, now musing in His thought,
A heauenly volie of light angels flew,
And from His Father Him a banquet brought,

---

1 = Presumption and Satan. G.

Through the fine element; for well they knew,
After His Lenten fast He hungrie grew;
   And, as He fed, the holy quires combine
   To sing a hymne of the celestiall Trine;
All thought to passe, and each was past all thought
     divine.

62.

The birds' sweet notes, to sonnet out their ioyes,
Attemper'd to the layes angelicall;
And to the birds, the winds attune their noyse,
And to the winds, the waters hoarcely call,
And Eccho back againe revoyced all;
   That the whole valley rung with victorie.
   But now our Lord to rest doth homeward flic:
See how the Night comes stealing from the moun-
     tains high!

CHRIST'S
TRIVMPH OVER DEATH.

THE ARGUMENT.

Christ's tryumph ouer death on the crosse, exprest. I. In generall
bv His ioy to vndergoe it, singing before He went to the garden :
Matt xxvi 30, st. 1—3—by His griefe in the vndergoing it : st.
4—6—by the obscure fables of the Gentiles typing it: st. 7—8—by
the cause of it in Him, His loue : st. 9—by the effect it should
haue in us : st. 10—12—by the instrument the cursed tree : st. 13—
1—II. Exprest in particular : 1. By His fore-passion in the
garden : st. 14—25—by His passion it selfe amplified. (1.) From
the general causes : st. 26—27 : parts, and effects of it : st. 28—29.
(2.) From the particular causes : st. 30—31 parts, and effects
of it—in heauen : st. 32—36—in the heauenly spirits : st. 37—
in the creatures sub-celestiall: st. 38—in the wicked Iewes : st.
39—in Iudas: st. 40—51—in the blessed saints, Ioseph of
Arimathea, &c., st. 52—67.

CHRIST'S TRIVMPH OVER DEATH.

1.

So downe the siluer streames of Eridan,[1]
On either side bank't with a lilly wall,
Whiter then both, rides the triumphant swan,
And sings his dirge, and prophesies his fall,
Diuing into his watrie funerall:
　　But Eridan to Cedron must submit
　　His flowry shore; nor can he enuie it,
If when Apollo sings, his swans doe silent sit.

2.

That heau'nly voice I more delight to heare,
Then gentle ayres to breath, or swelling waues
Against the sounding rocks their bosomes teare,
Or whistling reeds, that rutty[2] Iordan laues,

---

1 Eden? There can be no reference to amber-yielding
　Eridanus.　G.

2 Query 'course'-forming Jordan? Dr. Richardson as
　before quotes under 'rut.'　G.

And with their verdure his white head embraues,
    To chide the windes, or hiuing bees, that flie
    About the laughing bloosms of sallowie,[1]
Rocking asleepe the idle groomes that lazie lie.

3.

And yet, how can I hear Thee singing goe,
When men incens'd with hate Thy death foreset ?
Or els, why doe I heare Thee sighing so,
When Thou inflam'd with loue, their life doest get,
That loue, and hate, and sighs, and songs are met ;
    But thus, and onely thus Thy loue did craue,
    To sende Thee singing for vs to Thy graue,
While we sought Thee to kill, and Thou sought'st
        vs to saue.

4.

When I remember Christ our burden beares,
I looke for glorie, but finde miserie ;
I looke for ioy, but finde a sea of teares ;
I looke that we should liue, and finde Him die ;
I looke for angels' songs, and heare Him crie :
    Thus what I looke I cannot finde so well ;
    Or rather, what I finde, I cannot tell,
These bankes so narrowe are, those streames so
        highly swell.

---

1 Willows : Cf. Dr Richardson as before, s.v.   G.

5.

Christ suffers, and in this His teares begin ;
Suffers for vs—and our ioy springs in this ;
Suffers to' death—here is His manhood seen ;
Suffers to rise—and here His Godhead is.
For man, that could not by himselfe haue ris,
  Out of the graue doth by the Godhead rise,
  And God, that could not die, in manhood dies,
That we in both might liue by that sweete sacrifice.

6

Goe, giddy braines, whose witts are thought so fresh,
Plucke all the flowr's that nature forth doth throwe,
Goe sticke them on the cheekes of wanton flesh ;
Poore idol (forc't at once to fall and growe)
Of fading roses, and of melting snowe !
  Your songs exceede your matter; this of mine
  The matter which it sings, shall make diuine :
The starres dull puddles guild, in which their
    beauties shine.

7.

Who doth not see drown'd in Deucalion's[1] name
(When earth his men, and sea had lost his shore)
Old Noah? and in Nisus'[2] lock, the fame

---

1 Ovid, *Met.* I. 260, &c. G.
2 Apollod. III., 15. § § 5, 6, 8. G.

Of Sampson yet aliue ; and long before
In Phaëthon's, mine owne fall I deplore :
   But he that conquer'd hell, to fetch againe
   His virgin widowe, by a serpent slaine,
Another Orpheus was then dreaming poets feigne:

8.

This taught the stones to melt for passion,
And dormant sea, to heare him, silent lie ;
And at his voice, the watrie nation
To flocke, as if they deem'd it cheape, to buy
With their owne deaths his sacred harmonie :
   The while the waues stood still to heare his song,
   And steadie shore wau'd with the reeling throng
Of thirstie soules, that hung vpon his fluent tongue.

9.

What better friendship then to couer shame ?
What greater loue then for a friend to die ?
Yet this is better to asself the blame ;[1]
And this is greater, for an enemie :
But more then this, to die, not suddenly,
   Nor with some common death, or easie paine,
   But slowely, and with torments to be slaine ;
O depth, without a depth, farre better scene, then
    saine![2]

---

1 Self-blame. G.   2 Said. G.

10.

And yet the Sonne is humbled for the slaue,
And yet the slaue is proude before the Sonne;
Yet the Creator for His creature gaue
Himselfe and yet the creature hasts to runne
From his Creator, and self-good doth shunne;
 And yet the Prince, and God Himselfe doth crie
 To man, His traitour, pardon not to flie:
Yet man his[1] God, and traytour doth his prince
 defie.

11.

Who is it sees not that he nothing is,
But he that nothing sees? What weaker brest,
Since Adam's armour fail'd, dares warrant his?
That, made by God of all His creatures best,
Strait made himselfe the woorst of all the rest:
 If any strength we haue, it is to ill;
 But all the good is God's, both pow'r and will:
The dead man cannot rise, though he himselfe
 may kill.

12.

But let the thorny Schools their punctualls
Of wills, all good, or bad, or neuter diss:[2]
Such ioy we gained by our parentalls,

---

1 Cattermole misprints 'is.' G. 2 = Discuss? G.

That good, or bad, whether I cannot wiss,
To call it a mishap or happy miss,
   That fell from Eden, and to Heau'n did rise :
   Albee the mitred card'nall more did prize
His part in Paris then his part in Paradise.[1]

13.

A tree was first the instrument of strife,
Whear Eue to sinne her soul did prostitute;
A tree is now the instrument of life,
Though ill that trunke and this faire body suit :
Ah, cursed tree ! and yet O blessed fruit ![2]
   That death to Him, this life to vs doth giue :
   Strange is the cure, when things past cure reviue,
And the Physitian dies, to make his patient liue.

---

1 A favourite monition of the Puritan Divinity, *e.g.*
  Thomas Brooks of Cardinal BORBONIVS : Cf. my edn.
  of BROOKS, Vol. IV, p. 55: and under BOURBON in
  Index. G.

2 Very pretty is S. Austin's remark upon this passage:
  [St. Luke XXIII., 43] " Christ," saith he, " in rescuing
  the poor thief upon the cross was but quits with the
  devil, for the devil took man from God out of the midst
  of Paradise; Christ takes this poor man from Satan,
  when he was no less than in the very jaws of hell.
  Satan ruined man on the forbidden tree, and Christ
  saves them on the cursed tree'. MARCH *in loco* quoted
  by FORD in the Gospel of St. Luke Illustrated. G.

14.

Sweete Eden was the arbour of delight,
Yet in his hony flowr's our poyson blew;
Sad Gethseman the bowre of balefull night,
Whear Christ a health of poyson for vs drewe,
Yet all our hony in that poyson grewe :
    So we from sweetest flowr's could sucke our
        bane,
    And Christ from bitter venome could againe
Extract life out of death, and pleasure out of
        paine.

15.

A man was first the author of our fall,
A man is now the author of our rise;
A garden was the place we perisht all,
A garden is the place He payes our price;
And the Old Serpent with a newe deuise,
    Hath found a way himselfe for to beguile :
    So he, that all men tangled in his wile,
Is now by one man caught, beguil'd with his
        owne guile.

16.

The dewie night had with her frostic shade
Immant'led all the world, and the stiffe ground
Sparkled in yce; onely the Lord, that made
All for Himselfe, Himselfe dissolvèd found :

Sweat without heat, and bled without a wound :
  Of heau'n, and earth, and God, and man forlore, [1]
  Thrice begging helpe of those whose sinnes He
    bore,
And thrice denied of those, not to denie had swore. [2]

17.

Yet had He beene alone of God forsaken,
Or had His bodie beene imbroyl'd alone
In fierce assault; He might, perhaps haue taken
Some ioy in soule, when all ioy els was gone ;
But that with God—and God to heau'n is flow'n ;
  And Hell it selfe out from her graue doth rise,
  Black as the starles night : and with them flies,
Yet blacker then they both, the sonne of blas-
  phemies.

---

1 Forlorn   lost: Dr. Richardson, as before, quotes
  Fletcher above. G.
2 Richardson and Cattermole change 'them' into 'one,'
  and, literally taken, the correction is admissible : but
  they overlook—as is commonly done—that all the disciples had made the same profession and promise with
  St. Peter, e g. St. Mark xiv., 31.. [St. Peter] "He
  spake the more vehemently, If I should die with Thee,
  I will not denie Thee in any wise. *Likewise also said they
  all.*"—By 'forsaking' Him and 'fleeing' they all

18.

As when the planets with vnkind aspect,
Call from her caues the meager pestilence;
The sacred vapour, eager to infect,
Obeys tho voyce of the sad influence,
And vomits vp a thousand noysome sents:
   Tho well of life, flaming his golden flood
   With the sicke ayre, fevers the boyling blood,
And poysons all the bodie with contagious food.

19.

The bold physitian, too incautelous,
By those ho cures himselfe is murderèd;
Kindnes infects, pitie is dangerous;
And the poore infant, yet not fully bred,
Thear whear ho should bo borne, lies burièd:
   So tho darke prince, from his infernall cell,
   Casts vp his grisely torturers of Hell,
And whets them to revenge, with this insulting
    spell:—

'denied their Lord, though only St. Peter's articulate
denial is told in detail. He indeed excelled the others,
for he 'followed' still, albeit 'afar off.' Hence Fletcher,
in the spirit, and looking deeper than Richardson,
Cattermole and the rest, is accurate. G.

20.

'See how the world smiles in eternall peace ;
While we, the harmles brats and rustie throng
Of night, our snakes in curles doe pranke and
    dresse :
Why sleep our drouzie scorpions so long ?
Whear is our wonted vertue to doe wrong ?
  Are we our selues ? or are we Graces growen ?
  The sonnes of hell or heau'n ? was neuer knowne
Our whips so ouer-moss't and brands so deadly
    blowne !

21.

' O long desired, neuer-hop't for howre,
When our Tormentour shall our torments feele !
Arme, arme, your selues, sad Dires[1] of my pow'r,
And make our Iudge for pardon to vs kneele :
Slise, launch, dig, teare Him with your whips of
    steele :
  My selfe in honour of so noble prize,
  Will powre you reaking blood, shed with the
    cries
Of hastie heyres,[2] who their owne fathers sacrifice.

---

1 Diræ, the Furies. · G.   2 Heirs. G.

22.

With that a flood of poyson, blacke as Hell,
Out from his filthy gorge the beast did spue,
That all about His blessed bodie fell,
And thousand flaming serpents hissing flew
About His soule, from hellish sulphur threw,
   And euery one brandish't his firie tongue,
   And woorming all about His soule they clung;
But He their stings tore out, and to the ground
    them flung.

23.

So haue I scene a rock's heroique brest,
Against proud Neptune, that his ruin threats,
When all his waues he hath to battle prest.
And with a thousand swelling billows beats
The stubborne stone, and foams, and chafes, and
    frets
   To heaue him from his root, vnmooued stand;
   And more in heapes the barking surges band,
The more in pieces beat, flie weeping to the strand.

24.

So may wee oft a vent'rous father see,
To please his wanton sonne, his onely ioy,
Coast all about, to catch the roving bee,
And stung himselfe, his busie hands employ
To saue the honie for the gamessme boy;

Or from the snake her rank'rous teeth erace,
Making his child the toothles serpent chace,
Or, with his little hands, her tum'rous [1] gorge
  embrace.

25,

Thus Christ Himselfe to watch and sorrow giues,
While deaw'd in heauie sleepe dead Peter lies :
Thus man in his owne graue securely liues,
While Christ aliue, with thousand horrours dies,
Yet more for theirs then His owne pardon cries :
  No sinnes He had, yet all our sinnes He bare ;
  So much doth God for others' euills care,
And yet so careles men for their owne euills are.

26.

See drouzie Peter, see whear Iudas wakes,
Whear Iudas kisses Him whom Peter flies :
O kisse more deadly then the sting of snakes !
False loue more hurtfull then true injuries !
Aye me ! how deerly God His seruant buies !
  For God His man at His owne blood doth hold,
  And man his God, for thirtie pence hath sold :
So tinne for siluer goes, and dunghill drosse for
  gold.

---

1 Southey misprints ' tim'rous.'   G.

27.

Yet was it not enough for sinne to chuse
A seruant, to betray his Lord to them;
But that a subiect must his king accuse.;
But that a pagan must his God condemne;
But that a Father must His Sonne contemne,
  But that the Sonne must His owne death desire;
  That prince and people, seruant and the Sire,
Gentil and Jewe, and He against Himselfe con-
    spire?

28.

Was this the oyle, to make thy saints adore Thee,
The froathy spittle of the rascall throng?
Are these the virges[1], that ar borne before Thee,
Base whipps of corde, and knotted all along?
Is this thy golden scepter against wrong,
  A reedie cane? is that the crowne adornes
  Thy shining locks, a crowne of spiny thornes?
Ar thease the angels' himns, the priests' blasphe-
    mous scornes?

29.

Who euer sawe Honour before asham'd;
Afflicted Majestie; debasèd Height;
Innocence guiltie; Honestie defam'd;

---

1 Rods, as before. G.

Libertie bound; Health sick; the sunne in night?
But since such wrong was offred vnto Right,
　　Our night is day, our sicknes health is growne
　　Our shame is veil'd: this now remaines alone
For vs: since He was ours that wee bee not our
　　　owne.

30.

Night was ordeyn'd for rest, and not for paine,
But they, to paine their Lord, their rest contemne;
Good lawes to saue what bad men would haue
　　　slaine,
And not bad iudges, with one breath, by them
The innocent to pardon, and condemne:
　　Death for reuenge of murderers, not decaie
　　Of guiltles blood: but now, all headlong sway
Man's murderer to saue, man's Sauiour to slaie.

31.

Fraile multitude! whose giddy lawe is list[1]
And best applause is windy flattering;
Most like the breath of which it doth consist,
No sooner blowne but as soone vanishing,
As much desir'd as little profiting;

---

1 Choice.　G.

That makes tho men that haue it oft as light
As those that giue it; which the proud inuite,
And feare ;—the bad man's friend, the good man's
    hypocrite.

32.

It was but now their sounding clamours sung,
' Blessed is He that comes from the Most High !'
And all the mountaines with ' Hosanna !' rung;
And nowe, ' Away with Him—away'! they crie,
And nothing can be heard but ' Crucifie! '
    It was but now, the crowne it selfe they saue
    And golden name of King vnto Him gaue ;
And nowe, no king, but onely Cæsar, they will haue.

33.

It was but now they gathered blooming May,
And of his armes disrob'd the branching tree,
To strowe with boughs and blossomes all Thy[1] way ;
And now the branchlesse truncke a crosse for Thee
And May dismai'd, Thy coronet must be :
    It was but now they wear so kind, to throwe
    Their owne best garments whear Thy feet
        should goe,
And now, Thy selfe they strip, and bleeding
    wounds they show.

---

1 Cattermole misprints 'the'   G.

34.

See whear the Author of all life is dying :
O fearefull day !   He dead, what hope of liuing ?
See whear the hopes of all onr liues are buying :
O chearfull day ! they bought, what feare of grieu-
    ing ?
Loue, loue for hate, and death for life is giuing :
  Loe, how His armes are stretcht abroad to grace
    thee,
  And, as they open stand, call to embrace thee !
Why stai'st Thou then, my soule ?   O flie, flie,
    thither, hast thee !

35.

His radious head, with shamefull thornes they
    teare,
His tender backe, with bloody whipps they rent,
His side and heart they furrowe with a spear,
His hands and feete, with riuing nayles they tent ;[1]
And, as to disentrayle His soule they meant,
  They iolly at his griefe, and make their game,
  His naked body to expose to shame,
That all might come to see, and all might see, that
    came.

---

1 Stretch : Dr. Richardson has overlooked this example. G.

26.

Whereat the heau'n put out his guiltie eye,   ·
That durst behold so execrable sight,
And sabled all in blacke the shadie skie;
And the pale starres, strucke with vnwonted fright,
Quenched their euerlasting lamps in night;
    And at His birth, as all the starres heau'n had
    Wear not enough, but a newe star was made,
So now, both newe and old and all, away did fade.

37.

The mazèd[1] angels shooke their fieric wings,
Readie to lighten vengeance from God's throne,
One downe his eyes vpon the manhood flings,
Another gazes on the Godhead : none
But surely thought his wits were not his owne;
    Some flew to looke if it wear very Hee
    But when God's arm vnarmèd they did see,
Albee they sawe it was, they vow'd it could not
    bee.

38.

The sadded aire hung all in cheerelesse blacke,
Through which the gentle windes soft sighing flewe,
And Iordan into such huge sorrowe brake,
(As if his holy streame no measure knewe,)

---

1 Southey misprints 'amazed.'   G.

That all his narrowe bankes he ouerthrewe;
  The trembling earth with horrour inly shooke,
  And stubborne stones, such griefe vnus'd to
    brooke,
Did burst, and ghosts awaking from their graues
  gan looke.

39.

The wise philosopher cried, all agast,
' The God of nature surely languishèd !'
The sad Centurion cried out as fast,
The Sonne of God, the Sonne of God was dead ;"[1]
The headlong Iew hung downe his pensiue head,
  And homewards far'd ; and euer, as he went,
  He smote his brest, half desperately bent ;
The verie woods and beasts did seeme His death.
  lament.

40.

The gracelesse traytour round about did looke
(He lok't not long, the deuill quickely met him)
To finde a halter, which he found, and tooke;
Onely a gibbet nowe he needes must get him ;
So on a wither'd tree he fairly set him.

And help't him fit the rope, and in his thought
A thousand furies with their whippes, he brought;
So thear he stands, readie to Hell to make his
   vault.

41.

For him a waking bloodhound, yelling loude,
That in his bosome long had sleeping layde ;
A guiltie conscience, barking after blood,
Pursued eagerly, ne euer stai'd
Till the betrayer's selfe it had betray'd.
  Oft chang'd he place, in hope away to winde;
  But change of place could neuer change his
    minde :
Himselfe he flies to loose, and followes for to finde.

42.

Thear is but two wayes for this this soule to haue,
When parting from the body, forth it purges ;
To fly to heau'n, or fall into the graue,
Where whippes of scorpions, with the stinging
   scourges,
Feed on the howling ghosts, and firie surges
  Of brimstone, rowle about the caue of night;
  Where flames doo burne, and yet no sparke of
    light,
And fire both fries and freezes the blaspheming
   spright.

43.

Thear lies the captiue soule, aye-sighing sore,
Reckoning a thousand yeares since her first bands;
Yet staies not theốr, but addes a thousand more,
And at another thousand neuer stands,
But tells to them the starres, and heapes the sands:
. And now the starres are told, and sands are
        runne,
    And all those thousand thousand myriads done,
And yet but now, alas! but now all is begunne.

44.

With that a flaming brand a furie catch't
And shooke, and tos't it rounde in his wilde
        thought:
So from his heart all ioy, all comfort snatch't
With eu'ry starre of hope; and as he fought[1]
(With present feare, and future griefe distraught)
    To flie from his owne heart, and aide implore
    Of Him, the more He giues, that hath the more,
Whose storehouse is the heauens, too little for his
        store:

---

1 I read 'fought:' but I am not sure that 'sought' is
not intended. G.

45.

'Stay wretch on earth,' cried Satan—'restles rest;
Know'st thou not Iustice liues in heau'n ; or can
The worst of creatures liue among the best:
Among the blessèd angels cursèd man ?
Will Iudas now become a Christian ?
　　Whither will Hope's long wings transport thy
　　　　minde ?
　　Or canst thou not thy selfe a sinner finde ?
Or cruell to thy selfe, wouldst thou haue Mercie
　　kinde ?

46.

'He gave thee life : why shouldst thou seeke to
　　slay Him?
He lent thee wealth : to feed thy avarice ?
He cal'd thee friend : what, that thou shouldst
　　betray Him ?
He kis't thee, though He knew His life the price ;
He wash't thy feet: shouldst thou His sacrifice ?
　　He gaue thee bread, and wine, His bodie, blood,
　　And at thy heart, to enter in He stood ;
But then I entred in, and all my snakie brood.[1]

---

1 Euripides, Bacch. 816, 954, &c.: Theocritus xxvi,
　　10.　G.

47.

As when wild Pentheus, growne madde with fear,
Whole troupes of hellish haggs about him spies;
Two bloodie suns stalking the duskie sphear,
And twofold Thebes runs rowling in his eyes ;
Or through the scene staring Orestes flies,
 With eyes flung back vpon his mother's ghost,
 That, with infernall serpents all embost,
And torches quencht in blood, doth her stern
 sonne accost :[1]

48.

Such horrid Gorgons, and misformèd formes
Of damnèd fiends, flew dauncing in his heart,
That, now, vnable to endure their stormes,
' Flie, flie,' he cries, ' thyselfe, what ere thou art,
Hell, hell, alreadie burnes in eu'ry part.'
 So downe into his torturer's armes he fell,
 That readie stood his funeralls to yell,
And in a clowd of night to waft him quick[2] to
 Hell.

49.

Yet oft he snach't, and started as he hung :
So when the senses halfe enslumb'red lie,

---

1 See Euripides, Sophocles, Aeschylus.   G.
2 Living, alive, as before.   G.

The headlong bodie, readie to be flung
By the deluding phansie, from some high
And craggie rock, recovers greedily,
   And clasps the yeelding pillow, halfe asleep
   And, as from heav'n it tombled to the deepe,
Feeles a cold sweat through euery trembling
     member creepe.

50.

Thear let him hang, embowellèd in blood,[1]
Thear neuer any gentle shepheard feed
His blessed flocks, nor euer heav'nly flood[2]
Fall on the cursed ground, nor holesome seed,
That may the least delight or pleasure breed :
   Let neuer Spring visit his habitation,
   But nettles, kixe,[3] and all the weedie nation,
With emptie elders grow : sad signes of desolation!

51.

Whear let the Dragon keep his habitance,
And stinking karcasses be throwne avaunt ;
Faunes, Sylvans, and deformèd Satyrs daunce,
Wild-cats, wolues, toads, and skreech-owles direly
    chaunt ;

---

1 Misprinted 'Whear'. G.
2 Richardson and Cattermole misprint 'food,' G.
2 Wild plum. G.

Thear euer let some restles spirit haunt,
  With hollow sound, and clashing cheynes, to
    scarr
  The passenger, and eyes like to the starr
That sparkles in the crest of angrie Mars afarr.

52.

But let the blessed deawes for euer showr
Vpon that ground, in whose faire fields I spie
The bloodie ensigne of our Sauiour : .
Strange conquest, whear the Conquerour must die,
And He is slaine, that winns the victorie !
  But He that liuing, had no house, to owe it,
  Now had no graue: but Ioseph must bestowe it:
O runne, ye saints apace, and with sweete flow'rs
    bestrowe it !

53.

And ye glad spirits, that now sainted sit
On your cœlestiall thrones, in beawtie drest,
Though I your teares recoumpt, O let not it
With after-sorrowe wound your tender brest,
Or with new griefe vnquiet your soft rest :
  Inough is me your plaints to sound againe
  That neuer could inough my selfe complaine :
Sing, then, O sing aloude, thou Arimathean
    swaine !

54.

But long he stood, in his faint arms vphoulding
The fairest spoile heau'n euer forfeited,
With such a silent passion griefe vnfoulding
That, had the sheete but on himselfe beene spread,
He for the corse might haue been buried
   And with him stood the happie theefe that stole
   By night his owne saluation, and a shole
Of Maries, drowned, round about him sat, in dole.

55.

At length (kissing His lipps before he spake,
As if from thence he fetcht againe his ghost)
To Mary thus, with teares, his silence brake:
' Ah, woefull soule ! what ioy in all our cost,
When Him we hould, we haue alreadie lost ?
   Once did'st thou loose thy Sonne, but found'st
      againe,
   Now find'st thy Sonne, but find'st Him lost and
      slaine.
Ay mee ! though He could death, how canst thou
      life sustaine ?

56.

' Whear ere, deere Lord, thy Shadowe houereth,
Blessing the place, wherein it deigns abide,
Looke how the Earth darke horrour couereth,
Cloathing in mournfull black her naked side,

Willing her shadowe vp to heau'n to glide,
    To see, and if it meet Thee wandring thear ;
    That so, and if her selfe must misse Thee hear,
At least her shadow may her dutie to Thee bear.

57.

'See how the sunne in day-time cloudes his face,
And lagging Vesper, loosing his late teame,
Forgets in heau'n to runne his nightly race;
But, sleeping on bright Oeta's[1] top, doeth dreame
The world a chaos is ; no ioyfull beame
    Looks from his starrie bowre, the heau'ns do
        mone,
    And trees drop teares, least we should greeue
        alone;
The windes haue learn't to sigh, and waters
    hoarcely grone.

58.

'And you, sweete flow'rs, that in this garden growe,
Whose happie states a thousand soules enuie !
Did you your owne felicities but knowe,
Yourselues, vnpluckt[2] would to his funerals hie—
You neuer could in better season die:

---

1 Mountain in south of Thessaly. G.
2 Southey misprints 'uppluck'd.' G.

O that I might into your places slide!
The gate of heau'n stands gaping in His side ;[1]
Thear in my soule shonld steale, and all her faults
    should hide.[2]

59.

' Are theas the eyes that made all others blind?
Ah! why ar they themselues now blemishèd?
Is this the face, in which all beawtie shin'd ?
What blast hath thus His flowers debellishèd ?
Ar these the feete that on the watry head
    Of the vnfaithfull ocean passage found?
    Why goe they now so lowely vnder ground,
Wash't with our woorthless tears, and their owne
    precious wound ?

60.

' One hem but of the garments that He wore
Could medicine[3] whole countries of their paine ;
One touch of this pale hand conld life restore ;
One word of these cold lips reuiue the slaine :

---

1 Cf. Hebrews x., 20. G.
2 "Rock of Ages! cleft for me
  Let me hide myself in Thee."—TOPLADY. G.
3 A Shakesperian word. See Cymbeline iv. 2, and
  Othello iii. 3. G.

Well, the blinde man, Thy Godhead might main-
    taine :
  What, though the sullen Pharises repin'd?
  He that should both compare, at length would
    finde
The blinde man onely sawe, the seers all wear
    blinde.

61.

' Why should they thinke Thee worthy to be
    slaine ?
Was it because Thou gau'st their blinde men eyes?
Or that Thou mad'st their lame to walke againe?
Or for Thou heal'dst their sick mens' maladies ?
Or mad'st their dumbe to speake, and dead to
    rise?
  O could all these but any grace haue woon,
  What would they not to saue Thy life haue
    done ?
The dumb man would haue spoke, and lame man
    would haue runne.

62.

' Let mee, O let me neere some fountaine lie,
That through the rocke heaues vp his sandie head;
Or let me dwell vpon some mountaine high,
Whose hollowe root and baser parts ar spread

On fleeting waters, in his bowells bred,
   That I their steames, and they my teares may
     feed :
Or, cloathed in some hermit's ragged weed,
Spend all my daies in weeping for this cursèd
    deed.

63.

' The life, the which I once did loue, I leaue ;
The loue, in which I once did liue, I loath ;
I hate the light, that did my light bereaue :
Both loue and life, I doe despise you both.
O that one graue might both our ashes cloath !
   A loue, a life, a light, I now obteine,
   Able to make my age growe young againe—
Able to saue the sick, and to reuiue the slaine.

64.

Thus spend we teares, that neuer can be spent,
On Him, that sorrow now no more shall see ;
Thus send we sighs, that neuer can be sent,
To Him that died to liue, and would not be,
To be thear whear He would.   Here burie we
   This heau'nly earth ; here let it softly sleepe,
   The fairest Sheapheard of the fairest sheep :'
So all the bodie kist, and homeward went to
    weepe.

65.

So home their bodies went, to seeke repose,
But at the graue they left their soules behinde :
O who the force of loue cælestiall knowes !
That can the cheynes of nature's self vnbinde,
Sending the bodie home without the minde:
　　Ah, blessed virgin ! what high angel's art
　　Can euer coumpt thy teares, or sing thy smart,
When euery naile that pierst His hand, did pierce
　　　thy heart ?

66.

So Philomel, perch't on an aspin sprig,
Weeps all the night her lost virginitie,
And sings her sad tale to the merrie twig,
'I hat daunces at such ioyfull miserie,
Ne euer lets sweet rest inuade her eye ;
　　But leaning on a thorne her daintie chest,
　　For feare soft sleepe should steale into her brest,
Expresses in her song greefe not to be exprest.

67.

So when the larke—poore birde ! afarre espi'th
Her yet vnfeather'd children (whom to saue
She striues in vaine) slaine by the fatall sithe,
Which from the medowe her greene locks doeth
　　　shaue,

That their warme nest is now become their graue;
  The wofull mother vp to heauen springs,
  And all about her plaintiue notes she flings,
And their vntimely fate most pittifully sings.

CHRIST'S
TRIVMPH AFTER DEATH.

THE ARGUMENT.

Christ's triumph after death, 1—In His Resurrection, manifested by
the effects in the creatures: st. 1—7.—In Himselfe: st. 8—12.—
In His Ascension into Heauen; whose ioyes are described: st.
13—16.—(1) By the access of all good, the blessed societie of
saints, angels, &c.: st. 17—19.—The sweete quiet and peace
inioyed under God: st. 20.—Shadowed by the peace we enioy
vnder our soueraigne: st. 21—26.—The beautie of the place:
st. 27.—The caritie[1] (as the Schoole calls it) of the saints bodies:
st. 28—31.—The impletion of the appetite: st. 32, 33.—The ioy of
the senses, &c.: st. 34.—(2) By the amotion of all euill: st. 35,
36.—By the access of all good againe: st. 37.—In the glorie of
the holie citie: st. 38.—In the beatificall vision of God: st, 39—
42.—And of Christ: st. 43. [seqq

---

1 Query, clarity?   G.

CHRIST'S TRIVMPH AFTER DEATH.

1.

Bvt now the second morning, from her bowre
Began to glister in her beames ; and nowe
The roses of the Day began to flowre
In th' easterne garden; for heau'ns smiling browe
Halfe insolent for ioy begunne to showe :
  The early sunne came liuely dauncing out,
  And the bragge lambes ranne wantoning about,
That heau'n and earth might seeme in tryumph
    both to shout.

2.

Th' engladded Spring, forgetfull now to weepe,
Began t' eblazon from her leauie bed ;
The waking swallowe broke her halfe-yeare's
    sleepe,
And euerie bush lay deepely purpurèd

With violets; the wood's late-wintry head
  Wide flaming primroses set all on fire,
  And his bald trees put on their greene attire,
Among whose infant leaues the ioyeous birds conspire.

3.

And now the taller sonnes (whom Titan warmes)
Of vnshorne mountaines, blowne with easie windes,
Dandled the morning's childhood in their armes,
And if they chaunc't to slip the prouder pines,
The vnder corylets¹ did catch the shines,
  To guild their leaues; sawe neuer happie yeare
  Such ioyfull triumph and triumphant cheare,
As though the aged world anew created wear.

4.

Say Earth, why hast thou got thee new attire,
And stick'st thy habit full of dazies red?
Seems that thou doest to some high thought aspire,
And some newe-found-out bridegroome mean'st to
      wed:
Tell me, ye trees, so fresh appareèd,
  So neuer let the spitefull canker wast you,
  So neuer let the heau'ns with lightening blast you,
Why goe you now so trimly drest, or whither hast
      you?

5.

Answer me, Iordan, why thy crooked tide
So often wanders from his neerest way,
As though some other way thy streame would slide,
And fain salute the place where something lay?
And you sweete birds, that, shaded from the ray,
　　Sit carolling and piping griefe away,
　　　The while the lambs to heare you daunce and
　　　　play,
Tell me, sweete birds, what is it you faine would
　　say?

6

And thou, fair spouse of Earth, that euerie yeare
Gett'st such a numerous issue of thy bride,
How chance thou hotter shin'st, and draw'st more
　　neere?
Sure thou somewhear some worthie sight hast
　　spide,
That in one place for ioy thou canst not bide:[1]
　　And you, dead swallowes, that so liuely now
　　Through the flit[2] aire your wingèd passage rowe,
How could new life into your frozen ashes flowe?

---

1. Southey misprints ' hide '   G.
2. Flitting=moving ?   G.

O

7

Ye primroses and purple violets,[1]
Tell me, why blaze ye from your leauie bed,
And wooe mens' hands to rent you from your sets,
As though you would somewhear be carrièd,
With fresh perfumes and velvets garnishèd?
 But ah! I neede not aske, t'is surely so,
 You all would to your Sauiour's triumphs goe:
There would ye all waaite and humble homage doe.

8.

Thear should the Earth herselfe with garlands
 newe
And louely flowr's embellishèd, adore:
Such roses neuer in her garland grewe,
Such lillies neuer in her brest she wore,
Like beautie neuer yet did shine before:
 Thear should the sunne another sunne behold,
 From whence himselfe borrowes his locks of gold,
That kindle heau'n, and earth with beauties mani-
 fold.

9.

There might the violet, and primrose sweet,
Beames of more liuely, and more louely grace,

---

1 Giles and Phineas Fletcher reserve their daintiest praise
for these flowers. See our Essay. G.

Arising from their beds of incense meet;
Thear should the swallowe see new life embrace
Dead ashes, and the graue vnheal[1] his face,
    To let the liuing from his bowels creepe,
    Vnable longer his owne dead to keepe :
There heau'n and earth should see their Lord
        awake from sleepe.—

10.

Their Lord, before by others iudg'd to die
Now Iudge of all Himselfe ; before forsaken
Of all the world, that from His aide did flie,
Now by the saints into their armies taken ;
Before for an vnworthie man mistaken,
    Nowe worthy to be God confest ; before
    With blasphemies by all the basest tore,
Now worshippèd by angels, that Him lowe
        adore.

11.

Whose garment was before indipt in blood,
But now imbright'ned into heau'nly flame,
The sunne it selfe outglitters, though he should
Climbe to the toppe of the celestiall frame,

---

1 Unveil or uncover. G.

And force the starres go[1] hide themselues for shame:
  Before, that vnder earth was burièd
  But nowe aboue[2] the heau'ns is carrièd,
And thear for euer 'by the angels heried![3]

12.

So fairest Phosphor, the bright morning starre,
But neewely washt in the greene element,
Before the drouzie Night is halfe aware,
Shooting his flaming locks with deaw besprent,
Springs liuely vp into the Orient,
    And the bright droue, flece't in gold, he chaces
    To drinke that, on the Olympique mountaine
        grazes,
The while the minor planets forfeit all their faces.

13.

So long He wandred in our lower spheare,
That heau'n began his cloudy starres despise,
Halfe enuious, to see on Earth appeare
A greater light then flam'd in his own skies:
At length it burst for spight, and out thear flies

---

1 Richardson, Southey and Cattermole misprint 'to.'   G.
2 Misprinted originally 'about': corrected to 'above' in
    1632 edn. G
3 Honoured, praised. G.

A globe of wingèd angels, swift as thought
That on their spotted feathers liuely caught
The sparkling Earth, and to their azure fields it
  brought.

14.

The rest, that yet amazèd stood belowe,
With eyes cast vp, as greedie to be fed,
And hands vpheld, themselues to ground did
  throwe :
So when the Troian boy was ravishèd,
As through th' Idalian woods they saie he fled.
  His aged gardians stood all dismai'd,
  Some least he should have fallen back afraid,
And some their hasty vowes and timely prayers
  said.

15.

' Tosse vp your heads, ye euerlasting gates, [1]
And let the Prince of glorie enter in !
At whose braue voly of sideriall States,
The sunne to blush and starres grow pale wear seene;

---

1 Dr. J. M. Neale in his "Hymns, chiefly Mediæval, on
  the Joys and Glories of Paradise" (1866) gives a selection of stanzas—beginning with this—from this 'Part'
  of Fletcher's poem, and pronounces them " perhaps the
  most beautiful original verses, in a strictly religious
  poem, which the English language posesses" and adds

When leaping first from Earth He did begin
  To climbe his angells wings : then open hang
  Your christall doores! so all the chorus sang
Of heau'nly birds, as to the starres they nimbly
    sprang.

16.

Hearke! how the floods clap their applauding hands,
  The pleasant valleyes singing for delight;
The wanton mountaines daunce about the lands,
  The while the fieldes struck with the heau'nly
    light,
Set all their flow'rs a smiling at the sight;
  The trees laugh with their blossoms, and the
    sound
Of the triumphant shout of praise, that crown'd
The flaming Lambe, breaking through Heau'n hath
    passage found.

17.

Out leap the antique patriarchs, all in hast,
To see the powr's of Hell in triumph lead,

---

further " The reader to whom this poem is new, will, I
think allow that nothing more exquisite was ever
written than the 5, 6, 7, 10, 12, and 13 stanzas as here
numbered : corresponding with 20, 28, 30, 33, 35 and
36 of the complete Poem. G.

And with small starres a garland intercha'st
Of oliue-leaues they bore, to crowne His Head,
That was before with thornes degloried :
    After them flewe the prophets, brightly stol'd
    In shining lawne, and wimpled manifold.
Striking their yuorie harpes, strung all in chords of
    gold.

18.

To which the saints victorious carolls sung,
Ten thousand saints at once ; that with the sound
The hollow vaults of heau'n for triumph rung :
The cherubins their clamours did confound
With all the rest, and clapt their wings around :
    Downe from their thrones the dominations flowe
    And at His feet their crownes and scepters
        throwe,
And all the princely soules fell on their faces lowe.

19.

·Nor can the martyrs' wounds them stay behind,
But out they rush among the heau'nly crowd,
Seeking their heau'n out of their heau'n to find,
Sounding their siluer trumpets out so loude,
That the shrill noise broke through the starrie
        cloude,
    And all the virgin soules, in pure arraie,
    Came dauncing forth, and making joyous plaie :
So Him they lead along into the courts of day.

20.

So Him they lead into the courts of day,
Whear neuer warre nor wounds abide Him more ;
But in that house eternall peace doth plaie,
Acquieting the soules that newe before, [1]
Their way to heav'n through their owne blood did
    skore,
   But now, estrangèd from all miserie,
   As farre as heau'n and earth discoasted lie,
Swelter[2] in quiet waues of immortalitie!

21.

And if great things by smaller may be ghuest,
So, in the mid'st of Neptune's angrie tide
Our Brita[i]n Island, like the weedie nest
Of true halcyon, on the waues doth ride,
And softly sayling skornes the water's pride :
   While all the rest, drown'd on the Continent
   Add tost in bloodie waues, their wounds lament,
And stand, to see our peace, as struck with woon-
    derment. [3]

---

1 Southey misprints ' besore ' G.
2 = Grow warm : Dr. Neale changes to
   ' They bathe in quiet waves of immortality '. G.
3 Misnumbered in edition of 1610 and also in those of
   1632 and 1640 as ' 20 ' (bis) : so that there appear to
   be only 50 stanzas while there actually are 51. G.

22.

The ship of France, religious waues doe tosse,
And Greec[e] it selfe is now growne barbarous;
Spain's children hardly dare the ocean crosse,
And Belge's field lies wast[e] and ruinous;
That vnto those, the heau'ns are invious,
   And vnto them, themselues ar strangers growne,
   And vnto these, the seas ar faithles knowne,
And vnto her, alas! her owne is not her owne.

23.

Here only shut we Ianus yron gates,
And call the welcome Muses to our springs,
And are but[1] pilgrims from our heav'nly states
The while the trusty Earth sure plentie brings,
And ships through Neptune safely spread their
     wings.
   Go blessed Island, wander whear thou please,
   Vnto thy God, or men, Heau'n, lands or seas:
Thou canst not loose thy way, thy king with all
     hath peace.

24.

Deere prince! thy subjects ioy, hope of their heirs,
Picture of Peace, or breathing image rather;
The certaine argument of all our pray'rs,

---

1 Southey misprints here 'put' for 'but'   G.

Thy Harrie's[1] and thy countrie's louley father ;
Let peace in endles ioyes for euer bath her ·
  .Within thy sacred brest, that at thy birth
    Brough'st her with thee from Heau'n, to dwell
      on Earth,
Making our Earth a Heau'n, and paradise of mirth.

25.

Let not my liege misdeem[2] these humble laies
As lickt with soft and supple blandishment,
Or spoken to disparagon his praise ;
For though pale Cynthia, neere her brother's tent,
Soone disappeares in the white firmament,
  And giues him back the beames before wear his ;
  Yet when he verges, or is hardly ris,
She the viue image of her absent brother is.

26.

Nor let the Prince of Peace, his beadsman blame,
That with his stewart dares his Lord compare,
And heau'nly peace with earthly quiet shame :
So pines to lowely plants compared ar,

---

1 =Henry's i. e. Prince Henry whose death was so
  lamented by the nation. G.

2 Southey misprints 'disdain' G.

And lightning Phœbus to a little starro :
  And well I wot, my rime, albeo vnsmooth
  Ne saies but what it meanes, no meanes but
    sooth,
Ne harmes tho good, ne good to harmefull person
    doth. [1]

27.

Gaze but vpon the house whear man embowr's ;
With flowr's and rushes paued is his way,
Whear all the creatures ar his scruitours ;
The windes do sweepe his chambers euery day ;
And cloudes doo wash his rooms ; the seeling
    gay,
  Starrèd aloft, the guilded knobs embraue :
  If such a house God to another gaue,
How shine those glittering courts, He for Himselfo
    will haue ?

28.

And if a sullen cloud, as sad as night,
In which the sunne may seeme embodied,

---

1 Cattermole drops, without marking tho omission, stanzas
  21, 22, 23, 24, 25 and 26. G.

Depur'd[1] of all his drosse, we see so[2] white
Burning in melted gold his wat'rie head,
Or round with yuorie edges siluerèd,
    What lustre super-excellent will He
    Lighten on those that shall His sunneshine see,
In that all-glorious court in which all glories be ?

29.

If but one sunne whith his diffusive fires,
Can paint the starres, and the whole world with
        light,
And ioy, and life into each heart inspires,
And eu'ry saint shall shine in heau'n, as bright
As doth the sunne in his transcendent might,
    (As faith may well beleeue what Truth once
        sayes)
    What shall so many sunnes' united rayes,
But dazle all the eyes that nowe in heau'n we
        praise ?

30.

Here let my Lord hang vp his conquering launce,
And bloody armour with late slaughter warme,
And looking downe on His weake militants,
Behold His saints, mid'st of their hot alarme

Hang all their golden hopes vpon His arme;
    And in this lower field dispacing wide,
    .Through windie thoughts, that would their
        sayles misguide,
Anchor their fleshly ships fast in His wounded sido.

31.

Here may the band, that now in tryumph shines,
And that (before they wear inuested thus)
In earthly bodies carried heauenly mindes,
Pitcht[1] round about in order glorious,
Their sunny tents, and houses luminous;
    All their eternall day in songs employing,
    Ioying their ende, without ende of their ioying,
While their Almightie Prince destruction is destroy-
       ing.

32.

Full, yet without satietie, of that
Which whetts, and quiets greedy appetite,
Whear neuer sunne did rise, nor euer sat;
But one eternall day, and endles light
Giues time to those whose time is infinite—
    Speaking with thought, obtaining without fee,
    Beholding Him whom neuer eye could see,
And magnifying Him that cannot greater be.

---

1 Cattermole misprints 'pitch' G.

33.

How can such ioy as this want words to speake ?
And yet what words can speake such ioy as this ?
Far from the world, that might their quiet breake.
Here the glad soules the face of beauty kisse ;
Powr'd out in pleasure, on their beds of blisse ;
   And drunke with nectar-torrents, euer hold
   Their eyes on Him, whose graces manifold
The more they doe behold, the more they would
   behold.

34.

Their sight drinkes louely fires in at their eyes,
Their braine sweete incense with fine breath
   accloyes,
That on God's sweating[1] altar burning lies ;
Their hungrie eares feede on their heau'nly noyse,
That angels sing, to tell their vntould ioyes ;
   Their vnderstanding, naked truth ; their wills
   The all, and selfe-sufficient Goodnesse, fills :
That nothing here is wanting, but the want of
   ills.

35.

No sorrowe nowe hangs clowding on their browe,
No bloodles maladie empales their face,

---

1 Neale changes to 'That on the heavenly'   G.

No age drops on their hayrs his siluer snowe,
No nakednesse their bodies doeth embase,
No pouertie themselues and theirs disgrace,
　No feare of death the ioy of life deuours,
　No vnchast sleepe their precious time deflowrs,
No losse, no griefe,　no change,　waite　on　their
　　wingèd hours.

36.

But now their naked bodies skorne the cold,
And from their eyes ioy lookes, and laughs at paine;
The infant wonders how he came so old,
The old man how he came so young againe;
Still resting, though from sleep they still refraine[1]
　Whear all are rich, and yet no gold they owe,[2]
　And all are kings, and yet no subjects knowe,
All full, and yet no time on foode they doe bestow.

37.

For things that passe are past : and in this field
The indeficient Spring no Winter feares;

---

1 Changed (probably by misprint) to 'restraine' in 1632
　edition.　G.

2 Own.　G.

3 DR. NEALE says here 'Ho is simply translating the
　'Nam transire transiit' of S. Peter Damiani': but this
　is preposterous.　Rich and glowing as his Hymn *de*

The trees together fruit and blossome yeild;
Th' unfading lilly leaues of siluer beares,
And crimson rose a skarlet garment weares ;
   And all of these on the saints' bodies growe,
   Not, as they woònt, on baser earth belowe :
Three riuers here, of milke, and wine, and honie,
   flowe

38.

About the holy citie rowles a flood
Of moulten chrystall, like a sea of glasse ;
On which weake streame a strong foundation
   stood :
On liuing diamounds the building was,
That all things else, besides itselfe, did passe : [1]
   Her streetes, instead of stones, the starres did
   paue,
   And little pearles, for dust, it seem'd to haue ;
On which soft-streaming manna, like pure snowe,
   did waue.

Gloria Paradisi is in other thoughts, he is poor and
faint in the antithetic-ideas so vividly worded by
Fletcher in this stanza and the context. The most
hasty comparison will prove this. G.

1 Sur-pass. G.

39.

In midst of this citie cælestiall,
Whear tho Eternall Temple should haue rose,
Light'ned tho Idea[1] Beatificall :
End, and beginning of each thing that growes ;
Whose selfe no end, nor yet beginning knowes ;
   That hath no eyes to see, nor ears to heare ;
   Yet sees, and heares, and is all-eye, all-eare ;
That nowhear is contain'd, and yet is euery whear:

40.

Changer of all things, yet immutable ;
Before and after all, tho first and last ;
That, moouing all, is yet immoueable ;
Great without quantitie ; in Whose forecast
Things past are present, things to come are past ;
   Swift without motion ; to Whose open eye
   The hearts of wicked men vnbrested lie ;
At once absent and present to them, farre and
     nigh.[2]

---

1 Neale substitutes ' Vision.'   G.
2 Dr. Neale remarks ' One of our Poet's most careless
   lines.   Surely, something like this would have been
   better ?—
   " To whom the dark is light : to whom the far is nigh "
   but Fletcher's thought looks deeper.   G.

41.

It is no flaming lustre, made of light ;
No sweet concent, or well-tim'd harmonie ;
Ambrosia, for to feast the appetite,
Or flowrie odour, mixt with spicerie ;
No soft embrace, or pleasure bodily ;
   And yet it is a kinde of inwarde feast,
   A harmony, that sounds within the brest,
An odour, light, embrace, in which the soule doth
    rest.

42.

A heav'nly feast, no hunger can consume ;
A light vnseene, yet shines in euery place ;
A sound, no time can steale ; a sweet perfume
No winds can scatter ; an intire embrace
That no satietie can ere vnlace :
   Ingrac't into so high a fauour, thear
   The saints, with their beawpeers[1] whole world
    outwear ;
And things vnseene doe see, and things vnheard
   doe hear.

43.

Ye blessed soules, growne richer by your spoile ;
Whose losse, though great, is cause of greater gains ;

---

1 Beau-pere=companion : Cf. Spenser F.Q. III. 1. 35. G.

Here may your weary spirits rest from toyle,
Spending your endlesse cav'ning that remaines,
Among those white flocks and celestiall traines,
    That feed vpon their Sheapheard's eyes, and
        frame
That heau'nly musique of so woondrous fame,
Psalming aloude the holy honours of His name![1]

44.

Had I a voice of steel to tune my song,
Wear euery verse as smoothly fil'd as glasse,[2]
And euery member turnèd to a tongue,
And euery tongue wear made of sounding brasse;
Yet all that skill, and all this strength, alas!
    Should it presume to guild[3] wear misadvis'd,
    The place, where Dauid hath new songs devis'd,
As in his burning throne he sits emparadis'd.

---

1 Dr. Neale adds here "He is thinking no doubt of the
    Vesper Hymn:
              Largire clarum vespere
              Quo vita nunquam decidat:
    both Poets, of course drawing their inspiration from
    Zech. xiv. 7." **G.**

2 Southey has 'smooth as smoothest glass' **G.**

3 He substitutes 't' adorn' **G.**

45.

Most happie prince, whose eyes those starres behold,
Treading ours vnder feet! now maist thou powre
That ouerflowing skill, whearwith of ould
Thou woont'st to combe[1] rough speech; now
    maist thou showr
Fresh streames of praise vpon that holy bowre,
  Which well we Heaven call; not that it rowles
  But that it is the hauen of our soules—
Most happie prince, whose sight so heau'nly sight
    behoulds!

46.

Ah, foolish sheapheards, that wear woont esteem
Your god all rough and shaggy-hair'd to bee;
And yet farre wiser, sheapheards then ye deeme;
For who so poore (though who so rich) as hee
When, with vs hermiting[2] in lowe degree,
  He wash't His flocks in Jordan's spotles tide;
    And, that His deare remembrance aie might bide,[3]
Did to vs come, and with vs liu'd, and for vs di'd?

---

1 Here also he has 'smooth'   G.
2 Southey reads 'When sojourning with us in low degree'
  Richardson and Cattermole 'When with us sojourning
  in low degree'   G.
3 The same mis-read 'And that his dear remembrance
  might abide'   G.

47.

But now so liuely colours did embeame
His sparkling forehead, and so[1] shiny rayes
Kindled his flaming locks, that downe did stream
In curles along his necke, whear sweetly playes
(Singing His wounds of loue in sacred layes)
    His deerest Spouse,[2] Spouse of the deerest Louer,
    Knitting a thousand knots ouer and ouer,
And dying still for loue; but they her still recover:—

48.

Faire Egliset,[3] that at his eyes doth dresse
Her glorious face; those eyes from whence ar shed
Infinite belamours;[4] whear, to expresse
His loue, High God all heav'n as captive leads,
And all the banners of His grace dispreads,
    And in those windowes doth His armes englaze,
    And on those eyes the angels all doe gaze,
And from those eies the light of heau'n doe gleane[5]
    their blaze.

---

1 Southey misprints 'such'   G.
2 The Church.   G.
3 Richardson, Southey, and Cattermole substitute 'Fairest of Fairs.'   G.
4 Southey reads 'attractions infinite:'   =   attractions or love-spells.   G.
5 Southey reads 'obtain,' and Richardson and Cattermole 'catch.'   G.

69.

But let the Kentish lad,[1] that lately taught
His oaten reed the trumpet's siluer sound—
Young Thyrsilis, and for his musique brought
The willing sphears from hcau'n to lead a round
Of dauncing nymphs and heards,[2] that sung, and
    crown'd
  Eclecta's Hymen with ten thousand flowrs
    Of choycest prayse; and hung her heau'nly
    bow'rs
With saffron garlands, drest for nuptiall para-
    mours ;—

50.

Let his shrill trumpet with her siluer blast,
Of faire Eclecta and her spousall bed,
Be the sweet pipe, and smooth encomiast : .
But my greene Muse, hiding her younger head
Vnder old Chamus' flaggy banks, that spread
  Their willough locks abroad, and all the day
  With their owne watry shadowes wanton play—
Dares not those high amours, aud loue-sick songs
    assay.

---

1 Phineas Fletcher.—See our Memorial-Introduction,
  ante. G.
2 Richardson and Cattermole read ' swains.' G.

51.

Impotent words, weake lines,[1] that striuc in vaine—
In vaine, alas! to tell so heau'nly sight!—
So[2] heav'nly sight, as none can greater feigne,
Feigne what he can, that seemes of greatest might :
   Might any yet compare with infinite ?
Infinite sure those ioyes, my words but light ;
Light is the palace where she dwells—O blessed
   wight ![3]

---

1 Misprinted 'sides' in 1610 edn., and which Southey
  repeats. G.

2 Southey here, by misprinting 'To' for 'so,' and in line
  5th 'could' for 'might' misses the echoing repetition—
  a device afterwards used by Milton. See our Memorial-
  Introduction of Phineas Fletcher. G.

3 Richardson and Southey read 'O then how bright.' G·

Ruina cœli pulchra : iam terris decus,
Deusque : proles matris innuptæ, et pater :
Sine matre natus, sine patre excrescens caro :
Quem nec mare, æther, terra, non cœlum capit,
Vtero puellæ totus angusto latens ;
Æquævus idem patri, matre antiquior :
Heu domite victor, et triumphator ; tui
Opus opifex. qui minor quam sis, eo
Maior resurgis : vita, quæ mori velis,
Atq ergo possis ; passa finem Æternitas.
Quid tibi rependam, quid tibi rependam miser ?
Vt quando ocellos mollis inuadit quies,
Et nocte membra plurimus Morpheus premit,
Auide videmur velle de tergo sequens
Effugere monstrum, et plumbeos frustra pedes
Colerare ; media succidimus ægri fuga ;
Solitum pigrescit robur, os quærit viam,
Sed proditurus moritur in lingua sonus :
Sic stupeo totus, totus hæresco, intuens
Et sæpe repeto, forte si rependerem :
Solus rependit ille, qui repetit bene.

G. FLETCHER.

Τέλειον ἔστι, καὶ τελῶν Θεὸς τέλος.*

---

*In 1632 there follows here
Ἐστι τελῶν τὸ τέλος· τελος ἔστι Θεὸς τὸ τέλειον. G.

APPENDIX.

APPENDIX.

ENGRAVINGS IN THE RE-ISSUE OF 2ND EDITION (1632) IN 1640.

1.   The Birth of Christ—opposite page 1.   At bottom these lines :—

A new way here that prophets text may pass
for truth : the oxe his owner knew, the ass
his master's crib : thus thus incradled lay
your King, your Lord, your Christ : there fix, there
    stay
thy stoopinge, low, deiiected thoughts ; shall I
since he lay thus depressd, care where I lie.
                                            Esay 1. 3.

2.   The Circumcision of Christ—opposite page 23. At bottom these lines :—

View well this sacred portraiture, and see
what pangs thy Sauio[or] felt, and all for these :
Wilt thou returne a sacrifice may please
him who had felt all this ? be then all these :
Be thou both preist and knife : re-act each part
thy selfe againe, Go circumcise thy heart.

3. The Baptism of Christ—opposite page 26.   At
    bottom these lines :—

> How many riddlinge thoughts strangly appeare
> Unfolded in this shadow: for first here
> I see the Fountaine in the Streams: I see
> the water wa[s]hd by washing in't : And wee
> through nature black to pitch and inck, are scour'd
> to snow, while water's on an other pour'd
> I see againe.   Ile not say all I can
> least I turne Jordan to an ocean.

4. The Temptation of Christ—opposite page 30.
    At bottom these lines :—

> 'Tis written : Thus the tempter taught: (and thus
> by Scriptures wrack'd he oft preuailes on vs
> weake flesh and blood) But that he thus did dare
> By Moses and the prophets to insnare
> the sonne of God ; thinck it not strange that he
> become confounded in his policie
> for sure it could but slender hopes'afford
> he by the Scriptures should orecome ye Word.

5. The Crucifixion of Christ—opposite page 49.
    At bottom these lines :—

> What you see here does but the picture show
> of sorrowes picture : miracle of woe !
> Greefe was miscall'd till now: what plaints before
> e're mou'd the bowells of the earth or toare
> the rocks? nay more, the heaun's put out their light

And truc'd with darkness to auoide that sight.
Blind Israel! this this your hardnoss shewes
ye then turn'd stones whilst thus those stones turn'd
Jewes.

6. The Resurrection of Christ—opposite page 69.
At bottom these lines :—

Forget those horrid stiles of death : see here
who died, and by his presence there
imbalm'd the graue. See here who rose : and so
left hell infeebled, and the powers below
and death suppress'd. So that a child (no doubt)
may safly play wtht now the sting's pluck'd out

7. The Ascension of Christ—opposite page 81. At
bottom these lines :—.

Tis finish'd : and hees now gon vp on high
rich in the spoyles of hell : in maiesty,
and glorie (and glorie glorious farre
above all words) each glimpse treads out a starre,
dazles the sun : And whether true this bee
here written, follow him, and you shall see.

'Geo. Yate' is the 'sculpt[or]' of these 'engravings'
which are grotesque in the extreme, though in the
'Baptism' and 'Ascension' there are evident remin-
scenes of the great sacred Painters. Everywhere
perspective and proportion are violated.—The 'Temp-

tation' is ludicrous in its attempt to group the three temptations together. Generally the faces are hideous. It is just possible that as these Engravings did not appear until 1640 and so were posthumous, the Verses may belong to Phineas not Giles: but their place seems appropriate in Giles' volume. G.

A CANTO VPON THE DEATH OF ELIZA.*

HE early Howres were readie to unlocke
    The doore of Morne, to let abroad the
        Day;
When sad Ocyroe sitting on a rocke,
    Hemmed[1] in with teares, not glassing as they
        say
    Shee woont, her damaske beuties (when to
        play
Shee bent her looser fancie) in the streame,

---

* Originally published in 'Sorrowe's Joy, or a Lamen-
tation for our Deceased Soveraigne Elizabeth, with a
Triumph for the Prosperous succession of our Gratious
King James. Printed by John Legat, printer to the
University of Cambridge, 1603.' Our text is taken
from Nichol's 'Progresses of James I.,' Vol. I., pp.
17—19. In the margin are variations from the reprint[t]
in Nichol's 'Progresses of Queen Elizabeth,' Vol. III.,
257—259. G.

1 Hemmd. G.

That sudding[1] on the roeke, would closely seeme
To imitate her whitenesse with his frothy creame.

But hanging from the stone her carefull head,
    That shewed (for griefe had made it so to shew)
A'stone itselfe, that only differèd,
    That those without, these streamés within,
        did flow,
    Both euer ranne; yet neuer lesse did grow;
And tearing from her head her amber haires,
Whose like or none, or onely Phœbus weares,
Shee strowd them on the flood to waite vpon her
        teares.

About her many Nymphs sate weeping by,
    That when shee sang were woont to daunce
        and leape;
And all the grasse that round about did lie,
    Hung full of teares, as if that meant to weepe;
    Whilst th' vndersliding streames did softly
        creepe,
And clung about the rocke with winding wreath,
To heare a Canto of Elizae's[2] death;
Which thus poore nymph shee sung, whilest
        Sorrowe lent her breath.

---

1 Query—foaming, as in frothy (soap) ' suds?' G.
2 Elizaes. G.

Tell me, ye blushing currols that bunch out,
    To cloath with beuteous red your ragged sire [1]
    To let the sea-greene mosse curle round about,
      With soft embrace (as creeping vines do wyre
     Their loved elmes) your sides in rosie tyre;
So let the ruddie vermeyle of your cheeke
Make stain'd carnations fresher liueries seeke,
So let your braunched armes grow crooked, smooth,
    and slecke.

So from your growth late be you rent away,
    And hung with silver bels and whistles shrill;
Vnto those children be you giuen to play,
    Where blest Eliza raign'd; so neuer ill
    Betide your caues, nor them with breaking
     spill;
Tell me if some vncivill hand should teare
Your branches hence, and place them otherwhere;
Could you still grow, and such fresh crimson
    ensignes beare?

Tell me, sad Philomele, that yonder sits't
    Piping thy songs vnto the dauncing twig,
And to the waters fall thy musicke fit'st;
    So let the friendly prickle never digge

---

1 Misprinted 'fire' in Prog. of King James.   G.

Q

Thy watchfull breast with wound, or small,
　　or bigge,
　Whereon thou lean'st ; so let the hissing snake,
Sliding with shrinking silence, neuer take
Th' vnwarie foote, whilst thou perhaps hangst
　　half[1] awake.

So let the loathèd lapwing, when her nest
　Is stolne away, not as shee vses, flie,
Cousening the searcher of his promis'd feast,
　But, widdow'd of all hope, still *Itis* crie,
　And nought but *Itis*, *Itis*, till shee die.
Say, sweetest querister of the airie quirè,
Doth not thy Tereu, Tereu, then expire,
When Winter robs thy house of all her greene
　　attire ?

Tell me, ye veluet-headed violets
　That fringe the crooked banke, with gawdie
　　blewe ;
So let with comely grace your pretie[2] frets
　Be spread ; so let a thousand[3] *Zephyrs* sue
　To kisse your willing heads, that seeme t'
　　eschew
Their wanton touch with maiden modestie ;
So let the siluer dewe but lightly lie,
Like little watrie worlds within your azure skie.

---

1 Halfe.　G.　　2 Prettie.　G.　　3 Thousand.　G.

So when your blazing leaues aro broadly spread,
  Let wandring nymphes gather you in their
    lapps,
And send you whero Eliza lieth dead,
 ·To strow tho sheete that her pale bodie
    wraps;
  Aie me, in this I enuie your good haps;
Who would not die, there to be buried?
Say if the sunne denie his beames to shedde
Vpon your liuing stalkes, grow you not witherèd?

Tell me, thou wanton brooke, that slipst away
  T' avoid the straggling banks still flowing cling
So let thy waters cleanely tribute pay,
  Vnmixt with mudde, vnto the sea your king;
  So neuer let your streames leaue murmuring,
Vntil they steale by many a secret furt[1]
To kisse those walls that built Elizaes Court,
Drie you not when your mother springs are choakt
    with durt?

Yes, you all say, and I say, with you all,
  Naught without cause of ioy can ioyous bide,
Then me, vnhappie nymph, whom the dire fall
  Of my ioyes spring:—but there, aye mee,
    shee cried,

And spake no more; for sorrow speech denied,
And downe into her watrie lodge did goe;
The very waters when shee sunke did showe
With many wrinkled[1] ohs, they sympathiz'd her
   woe:

The sunne in mourning clouds inveloped,
   Flew fast into the westearne world to tell
Newes of her death; Heaven it selfe sorrowed
   With teares that to the earthes dank bosome
   fell;
But when the next Aurora 'gan to deale
Handfuls of roses 'fore the teame of day,
A shepheard[2] droue his flocke by chance that
   way,
And made the nymph to dance that mournèd
   yesterday.

             G. FLETCHER, Trinit.

---

1 Wrinckled. G.   2 Sheappheard. G.

REWARD OF THE FAITHFULL.*

(1.) THE HEAVENLY COUNTRY.

.... "Which diuine thought wee shall not find in the hearts alone of the children of light, that haue the starres of heauen shining thicke in them, (Hebr. 11, 16) but in the minds of heathen men, that lay shadowed in their owne naturall wisedome, out of which the banisht Consul of Rome, Boetius could sing

> Hæc, dices, memini patria est mihi,
> Hinc ortus, hic sistam gradum.
> O this my country is, thy soule shall say,
> Hence was my birth, and here shall be my stay."

(pp. 29, 30.)

[Boethius, Cons. Phil. IV., metr. 1, l. 25, 26. G.]

---

* See our Memorial-Introduction for account of the Treatise. G.

(2.) THE ROSE and 'BLACK BUT COMELY.'

"Cleane opposite are these glories, and delights, and this ambition to those of our vnder-world. Gather all the roses of pleasure that grow vpon the earth, sayes not the Greek Epigram truely of them:

Τὸ ῥόδον ἀκμάζει βαιὸν χρόνον, ἢν δὲ παρέλθῃ,
ζητῶν εὑρήσεις οὐ ῥόδον, ἀλλὰ βάτον.

> The Rose is faire and fading, short and sweet,
>   Passe softly by her:
> And in a moment you shall see her fleet,
>   And turne a bryer.

They looke fairely, but they are sodainely dispoiled: whereas, contrary, all the flowers of Paradise (like the Church, *Cant.* I. 5. 6.) sun-burnt and frosted with the heat and cold of this tempestuous world, looke black and homely, but flourish inwardly with · diuine beauty, and are all glorious within. So that wee may well say of the Church as the Poet sings:—

> She's black: what then? so are dead coales, but cherish,
>   And with soft breath them blow,
> And you shall see them glow as bright and flourish,
>   As spring-borne Roses grow.   (pp. 120, 121.)

[The author of the Epigram Rose seems unknown: but Jakobs gives a German translation as follows:—

"Wenige Tage nur währt die Rosenzeit; sind sie ver-
schwunden,
Siehst du die Rose nicht mehr; sondern die Dornen
allein."

Dr. Johnson quotes it in his 'Rambler,' No. 71, with the
sole difference of $\pi a \rho \acute{\epsilon} \lambda \theta \eta s$ for the last word of the
first line : which elsewhere occurs as $\pi a \rho \acute{\epsilon} \lambda \theta \eta$ (as in
Fletcher). Johnson gives no author's name but trans-
lates

"Soon fades the rose; once past the fragrant hour,
The loiterer finds a bramble for a flower."

[See Notes and Queries, 4th. S. 11th April, 1868 : p. 351.
and Anthologia Græca, IV. 126, ed. Jacobs.]
A Correspondent of 'Notes and Queries' with reference
to the Epigram, communicates an amusing Greek pun
from it, which he heads 'Cane and Birch.'—"The
occasion of it was a complaint of a friend to an old-
fashioned pedagogue that, objecting to the corporal
punishment of little boys at school, he had sent his
son to one where it was said *birch* was unknown, but
found that a very cruel and severe use of *the cane* was
substituted for it. Ah !" said the old-fashioned
school-master exultingly, whose meditations, like
Fielding's Thwackum's, were full of birch,

$Z\eta\tau\hat{\omega}\nu\ \acute{\epsilon}\upsilon\rho\acute{\eta}\sigma\epsilon\iota s\ o\grave{\upsilon}$ 'POΔON $\grave{a}\lambda\lambda\grave{a}$ BATON.

The reply was pedantic, but it was appropriate. [As
before, May 16th, p. 467.]
Perhaps it may be well to remember on the whole, the
fine words of Dr. F. W. Faber :—"Roses grow on

briars, say the wise men of the world, with that
sententious morality which thinks to make virtue
truthful by making it dismal. Yes! but as the very
different spirit of piety would say, it is a truer truth
that briars bloom with roses. If roses have thorns,
thorns also have roses. This is the rule of life. Yet
everybody tells us one side of this truth, and nobody
tells us the other."—("The Precious Blood," p. 216.)
The second Epigram *supra*, is too corruptly given in the
Greek (by Fletcher) for restoratiou: and too unimpor-
tant to spend pains on. G.]

(3.) THE RICH POOR MAN.

" Let vs graunt Diues the happinesse to die a
rich man, which he shall neuer doe (for as the
heathen sings of death,

Involuit humile pariter et celsum caput.
Æquatque summis infima.
Death and the Graue, make euen all estates.
There, high, and low, and rich, and poor are mates."
                                        (p. 203.)*
[Boethius: De Cons. Phil. lib. ii., metr. 7, 1. 13 14. G.]

(4.) UNGODLY RICH.

"To speake soothly, as the last of the best, and the
best of the last, Poets saies of all morall helpes

---

* LIVESEY (as before) gives this more tersely :—
    ' There is no difference: Death hath made,
    Equal the sceptre and the spade.'   (p. 66.)   G.

which Fabricius, and Cato, and Brutus, three of
the most famous of the Romane Worthies thought
to eternize themselues by,

> Cum sera vobis͵rapiet hoc etiam dies,
> Iam vos secunda mors manet:

So may the vngodly rich more truly say of himselfe, and all worldly meanes, whereby he hoped to
perpetuate* his life and memorie.

> The poor man dies but once: but O that I
> Already dead, haue yet three deaths to die.

For, being dead in his bodie, he still remaines aliue
in his soule, estate, and posteritie to suffer death,
and therefore death is said *to gnaw, and feed
vpon him*. Psal. 49. 14. (p. 205-207.)" [Boethius
is the poet referred to, *supra*: De Cons: Phil: lib ii.
metr. 7, 1. 25, 26.   G.]

(5.) THE 'GODS' ACCUSED.

"Neither did simple women onely, but the wisest
of the heathen Gouernors loade their Gods with
their proper crimes:

> ——ἐγὼ δ' οὐκ αἴτιός εἰμι,
> Ἀλλὰ Ζεὺς καὶ μοῖρα καὶ ἠεροφοῖτις Ἐρινύς.

---

* Misprinted 'perpetrate'   G.

Sayes great Agamemnon, alas!

> It was not he that did them iniurie.
> But Ioue and Fate, and the night Furie.

But Iupiters answer is recorded by the same Poet:

> Ἐξ ἡμέων γάρ φασι κάκ᾽ ἔμμναι οἱ δὲ καὶ αὐτοὶ
> Σφῇσιν ἀτασθαλίῃσιν ὑπέρμορον ἄλγε᾽ ἔχουσιν.

Men say their faults are ours when their own wils
Beyond their fate, are authours of their ills." (pp. 232, 235.)
[Homer Iliad xix., 86, 87. and Od. i. 33, 34. G.]

(6.) HUSBANDRY.

"The Art of husbandry....wants both schóllers
and teachers, meeting, very seldom with such
religious votaries towards them as the Prince of the
Latin Poets was, who in his Georgicks, or Poeticall
Husbandrie, breaks out into this godly wish.

> Me vero primum dulces &c.
> No, first of all O let the Muses wings
> Whose sacred fountaine in my bosome springs,
> ᾽Receiue, and landing mee aboue the starres,
> Shew me the waies of heuen: but if the barres
> Of vnkinde nature stoppe so high a flight,
> The Woods and Fields shall be my next delight." (pp.
> 273, 274.)
>   [Virgil, Georg. ii., 475-478, 483, 485. G.]

(7.) OTHERS.

It is indeede the nature of al men to think other mens liues more happy then their owne,

Optat ephippia bos piger, optat arare caballus.
Faine would the Oxe the horses trappins weare;
And faine the Horse the oxes yoake would beare. (p. 283.)
[Horace Epist. i. 14, 43.   G.]